# The Essential Diabetic Cookbook

## for Beginners

Aurora August

## Copyright Statement:

© 2024 Aurora August. All rights reserved. No part of this book may be reproduced, stored, or transmitted in any form or by any means, electronic, mechanical, photocopying, recording, scanning, or otherwise, except as permitted under Section 107 or 108 of the 1976 United States Copyright Act, without the prior written permission of the publisher, except in the case of brief quotations embodied in critical reviews and certain other non-commercial uses permitted by copyright law.

For permission requests, write to the publisher at the address below:

amazon.cookbook96@gmail.com

## Disclaimer:

The information and recipes provided in this book are intended for informational purposes only. They are not intended to be a substitute for professional medical advice, diagnosis, or treatment. Always seek the advice of your physician or other qualified health provider with any questions you may have regarding a medical condition. Never disregard professional medical advice or delay in seeking it because of something you have read in this book.

The author and publisher of this book make no representation or warranties with respect to the accuracy, applicability, fitness, or completeness of the contents of this book. They refuse any warranties (expressed or implied), merchantability, or fitness for any particular purpose. The author and publisher shall in no event be held liable for any loss or other damages, including but not limited to special, incidental, consequential, or other damages.

amazon.cookbook96@gmail.com

# Table of contents

**Introduction** ................................................................................................... 6
Opening Statement ........................................................................................ 6
Purpose Of The Diabetic Diet ........................................................................ 6
Core Principles Of The Diabetic Diet ............................................................. 8
Cultural And Historical Background .............................................................. 10
Importance Of Adopting The Diabetic Diet .................................................... 12
Encouragement And Motivation .................................................................... 13

**1 - Getting Started** ........................................................................................ 15
Kitchen Essentials - Must-Have Tools And Appliances ................................. 15
Pantry Basics - Stocking Diabetic-Friendly Ingredients ................................. 16
Reading Labels - Understanding Nutritional Information ............................... 19
30 Food That Must Be Banned Or Limited For Diabetics .............................. 21
Moving Forward ............................................................................................ 22

**2 - Breakfast Boosters** ................................................................................. 23
Why Breakfast Matters: Importance Of A Healthy Start ................................ 23
    Scrambled Tofu With Vegetables ........................................................... 25
    Whole Grain Toast With Smashed Avocado And Tomatoes .................. 26
    Greek Yoghurt With Nuts And Fresh ...................................................... 27
    Quinoa Bowl With Berries And Nuts ...................................................... 28
    Cottage Cheese And Berry Parfait ......................................................... 29
    Vegetable Omelette With Mushrooms And Bell Peppers ...................... 30
    Oatmeal With Flaxseeds And Blueberries .............................................. 31
    Smoked Salmon And Cucumber Roll-Ups ............................................. 32
    Avocado And Spinach Smoothie ............................................................ 33
    Chia Seed Breakfast Bowl ...................................................................... 34

**Chapter 3 - Wholesome Lunches** ............................................................... 35
Balancing Macronutrients: Protein, Carbs, And Fats .................................... 35
    Grilled Chicken Salad With Mixed Greens And Vinaigrette ................... 38
    Quinoa And Black Bean Salad With Lime Dressing .............................. 39
    Turkey And Avocado Lettuce Wraps ...................................................... 40
    Lentil And Vegetable Soup ..................................................................... 41
    Spinach And Mushroom Stuffed Bell Peppers ....................................... 42
    Chickpea And Tuna Salad With Lemon Vinaigrette ............................... 43
    Baked Sweet Potato With Greek Yoghurt And Chives ........................... 44
    Zucchini Noodles With Pesto And Cherry Tomatoes ............................. 45
    Chicken And Vegetable Stir-Fry ............................................................. 46
    Tomato And Basil Soup With A Side Of Whole Grain Bread ................. 47

## 4 - Nutritious Dinner........................................................................................48
Planning Balanced Meals: Strategies For Dinner .............................................. 48
- Baked Salmon With Asparagus And Quinoa................................................ 50
- Grilled Chicken With Steamed Broccoli And Brown Rice ........................... 51
- Stir-Fried Tofu With Mixed Vegetables........................................................ 52
- Turkey Meatballs With Zucchini Noodles ................................................... 53
- Baked Cod With Roasted Brussels Sprouts ................................................. 54
- Vegetable Curry With Cauliflower Rice ....................................................... 55
- Lean Beef Stir-Fry With Bell Peppers And Snow Peas ................................ 56
- Herb-Crusted Pork Tenderloin With Green Beans ...................................... 57
- Stuffed Portobello Mushrooms With Spinach And Cheese ......................... 58
- Spaghetti Squash With Marinara And Turkey Meat Sauce ......................... 59

## 5 – Smart Snacking ............................................................................ 60
Healthy Snack Options: Managing Cravings .................................................... 60
- Hummus With Cucumber And Carrot Sticks .............................................. 62
- Apple Slices With Almond Butter................................................................ 63
- Greek Yoghurt With Walnuts And Fresh Berries ........................................ 64
- Roasted Chickpeas With Paprika ................................................................ 65
- Celery Sticks With Cottage Cheese ............................................................. 66
- Baked Kale Chips With Sea Salt .................................................................. 67
- Mixed Nuts And Dried Unsweetened Berries ............................................. 68
- Edamame With A Sprinkle Of Sea Salt ....................................................... 69
- Cherry Tomatoes And Mozzarella Balls ...................................................... 70
- Bell Pepper Slices With Guacamole............................................................. 71

## 6 – Delightful Desserts...................................................................... 72
Sugar Alternatives: Using Sweeteners Wisely ................................................... 72
- Dark Chocolate Avocado Mousse ................................................................ 74
- Baked Apple With Cinnamon And Walnuts................................................ 75
- Chia Seed Pudding With Coconut Milk ...................................................... 76
- Sugar-Free Lemon Cheesecake Bites........................................................... 77
- Raspberry Yoghurt Popsicles....................................................................... 78
- Almond Flour Chocolate Chip Cookie ........................................................ 79
- Berry Crumble With Oats And Almonds .................................................... 80
- Pumpkin Spice Energy Balls ....................................................................... 81
- Coconut Macaroons With Dark Chocolate Drizzle ..................................... 82
- Pears Poached In Red Wine With A Cinnamon Stick ................................. 83

## 7 - Meal Planning And Prep .................................................................................. 84
Weekly Meal Plans: Sample Plans For Beginners ................................................. 84
Shopping List ............................................................................................................. 86
Prep Tips: How To Efficiently Prepare Meals In Advance ..................................... 88

## 8 - Lifestyle Tips For Diabetics ............................................................................. 91
Exercise And Fitness: Incorporating Physical Activity ........................................... 91
Stress Management: Techniques For Reducing Stress .......................................... 93
Monitoring Progress: Keeping Track Of Health Metrics ....................................... 95

## Conclusion ............................................................................................................... 97
Understanding The Importance Of Support ........................................................... 97

## Appendices ............................................................................................................. 99
Basics Glossary Of Terms For The Diabetic Diet .................................................... 99
Measurement Conversions For The Diabetic Diet: A Beginner's Guide For The Uk ............ 102

## Index ...................................................................................................................... 106

# INTRODUCTION

## Opening Statement

Diabetes is an increasingly common condition in the UK, affecting millions of individuals and families. As its prevalence continues to rise, the effective dietary management has become paramount. The Diabetic Diet is a powerful tool designed to help manage blood sugar levels, improve overall health, and enhance the quality of life for those with diabetes.

This diet is not simply a list of do's and don'ts. It is a comprehensive approach to eating that emphasises balance, moderation, and mindful choices. The principles of the Diabetic Diet are grounded in modern nutritional science and enriched by cultural traditions, offering a comprehensive path to better health. By understanding and applying these principles, individuals can take control of their diabetes and work towards preventing its complications.

Throughout this book, you will explore the core components of the Diabetic Diet. You will learn about the significance of balanced macronutrients, the art of carbohydrate counting, and the benefits of being aware of the glycaemic index of foods. You will discover strategies for managing portion sizes, maintaining regular meal timings, and choosing healthy snacks that support stable blood sugar levels. Additionally, you will understand the importance of staying hydrated, limiting sugary foods, and practicing mindful eating. Finally, you will see why consulting with a dietitian is essential for tailoring the diet to individual needs.

Each of these principles is crucial for managing diabetes effectively. However, the benefits of the Diabetic Diet extend beyond those living with the condition. This way of eating provides a blueprint for a healthier lifestyle that can be embraced by anyone seeking to improve their dietary habits and overall well-being.

Adopting the Diabetic Diet is about more than just the food on your plate. It involves a commitment to a lifestyle that includes regular physical activity, enjoying meals with loved ones, and making informed choices that benefit both body and mind. As we delve into the specifics of the Diabetic Diet, approach this journey with an open mind and a cheerful outlook. The changes you make today can lead to a lifetime of health and vitality.

Welcome to the beginning of a healthier, more balanced life. Let us embark on this journey together, one informed and mindful step at a time.

## Purpose of the Diabetic Diet

The Diabetic Diet is a vital tool for managing diabetes, a condition that affects a massive portion of the population in the UK. With diabetes, the body's ability to regulate blood glucose levels is impaired, leading to potential complications if not effectively managed. The primary purpose of the Diabetic Diet is to help maintain stable blood sugar levels, thereby reducing the risk of these complications and promoting overall health.

## 1. Managing Blood Sugar Levels

At its core, the Diabetic Diet is designed to stabilise blood glucose levels. This is achieved by focusing on a balanced intake of macronutrients—carbohydrates, proteins, and fats. Carbohydrates have the most direct impact on blood sugar, so controlling the type and amount consumed is essential. By learning to count carbohydrates and understanding the glycaemic index (GI) of foods, individuals can make informed choices that prevent blood sugar spikes and dips.

Low-GI foods, such as whole grains, legumes, and non-starchy vegetables, cause a slower rise in blood sugar, making them preferable options. Regular monitoring and appropriate adjustments ensure that meals are both satisfying and blood sugar friendly.

## 2. Supporting Weight Management

Weight management is a critical aspect of diabetes care, particularly for those with Type 2 diabetes. Excess weight can increase insulin resistance, making blood sugar control more difficult. The Diabetic Diet encourages portion control and balanced meals, which can help with weight loss and maintenance. By choosing nutrient-dense foods that are lower in calories but high in essential 2 nutrients, individuals can achieve and maintain a healthy weight.

Regular meal timings and healthy snacking also play a role in preventing overeating and managing hunger. This structured approach to eating helps avoid the pitfalls of erratic eating patterns, which can lead to weight gain and poor blood sugar control.

## 3. Enhancing Cardiovascular Health

Diabetes is often associated with an increased risk of cardiovascular diseases, including heart attack and stroke. The Diabetic Diet promotes heart health by encouraging the consumption of healthy fats, lean proteins, and high-fibre foods. Reducing the intake of saturated fats and trans fats, while incorporating sources of omega-3 fatty acids, such as fish, nuts, and seeds, supports heart health and helps manage cholesterol levels.

Moreover, the emphasis on fruits, vegetables, and whole grains provides essential vitamins, minerals, and antioxidants that contribute to cardiovascular health. Limiting sugary foods and beverages further reduces the risk of developing heart-related issues.

## 4. Promoting Longevity and Quality of Life

Beyond managing diabetes and its associated risks, the Diabetic Diet aims to enhance overall well-being and longevity. A balanced, nutritious diet can lead to improved energy levels, better mood, and enhanced physical and mental performance. By adopting a lifestyle that includes regular physical activity and mindful eating, individuals can experience a higher quality of life.

Mindful eating involves paying attention to hunger and fullness cues, enjoying meals without distractions, and making thoughtful food choices. This practice not only helps control portions but also fosters a healthier relationship with food.

### 5.Tailoring to Individual Needs

One of the strengths of the Diabetic Diet is its flexibility and adaptability to individual needs. Working with a registered dietitian allows for personalisation based on factors such as age, activity level, medication, and personal preferences. A dietitian can provide tailored advice, helping individuals create meal plans that fit their lifestyle while effectively managing diabetes.

### 6.Encouraging a Holistic Approach

The Diabetic Diet is not just about the food consumed; it encompasses a holistic approach to health. Regular physical activity, stress management, and adequate sleep are all integral components of diabetes management. Combining these lifestyle factors with a balanced diet creates a comprehensive strategy for maintaining optimal health.

## Core Principles of the Diabetic Diet

The Diabetic Diet is built on a foundation of well-established principles designed to help manage blood sugar levels effectively. These principles are adaptable, allowing for personalised adjustments based on individual needs and preferences. Let us explore each core principle in detail and understand how they contribute to better diabetes management.

### 1. Balanced Macronutrients

A key aspect of the Diabetic Diet is ensuring a balanced intake of macronutrients: carbohydrates, proteins, and fats. Each plays a crucial role in maintaining energy levels and overall health.

- » Carbohydrates: These should make up about 45% of your daily calorie intake. For someone on a 2,000-calorie diet, this translates to 225 grams of carbohydrates per day. Women typically aim for 45 grams per meal, while men might aim for 60 grams per meal.
- » Proteins: Protein should account for about 25-30% of your daily calories. Sources like lean meats, fish, eggs, beans, and lentils are excellent choices.
- » Fats: Healthy fats should make up around 30-45% of your daily calories. Focus on unsaturated fats from sources like olive oil, nuts, seeds, and avocados.

### 2. Carbohydrate Counting

Carbohydrate counting is a vital skill for managing blood sugar levels. It involves keeping track of the number of grams of carbohydrates consumed at each meal and snack.

- » For Women: Typically, 45 grams of carbohydrates per meal.
- » For Men: Typically, 60-75 grams of carbohydrates per meal.
- » Snacks: Both men and women should aim for 15-30 grams of carbohydrates per snack.

Using tools like nutrition labels, food diaries, and mobile apps can simplify this process. By monitoring carbohydrate intake, you can prevent blood sugar spikes and ensure more stable glucose levels throughout the day.

### 3. Glycaemic Index Awareness

Understanding the glycaemic index (GI) of foods helps in selecting carbohydrates that have a slower, more gradual impact on blood sugar levels.

- » Low-GI Foods: Foods like whole grains, legumes, non-starchy vegetables, and most fruits have a low GI and are ideal choices.
- » Moderate-GI Foods: Foods such as whole wheat products and brown rice fall into this category and can be included in moderation.
- » High-GI Foods: Foods like white bread, sugary cereals, and processed snacks should be limited as they cause rapid spikes in blood sugar.

### 4. Portion Control

Portion control is crucial for managing calorie intake and preventing overeating. Tools like measuring cups, food scales, and portion control plates can help ensure appropriate serving sizes.

- » Visual Cues: A serving of meat should be about the size of a deck of cards, while a serving of pasta or rice should be about the size of a clenched fist.

### 5. Regular Meal Timing

Consistent meal timing helps maintain steady blood sugar levels. Irregular eating patterns can lead to fluctuations in blood glucose.

- » Meal Frequency: Aim for three main meals and 1-2 snacks per day.
- » Timing: Try to eat meals at the same times each day, 4-5 hours apart.

### 6. Healthy Snacking

Choosing healthy snacks helps maintain blood sugar levels between meals. Ideal snacks are high in fibre and protein and low in sugar.

- » Examples: Nuts, seeds, Greek yoghurt, vegetable sticks with hummus, and fruit with a small piece of cheese.

### 7. Hydration

Staying well-hydrated is important for overall health and can help control blood sugar levels.

- » Recommended Intake: Aim for at least 6-8 glasses of water per day. Herbal teas and drinks without added sugars also contribute to hydration.

### 8. Limiting Sugary Foods

Reducing the intake of foods and drinks high in added sugars is essential for blood sugar control.

- » Avoid: Sugary beverages, sweets, cakes, and biscuits.
- » Alternative: Use natural sweeteners like stevia or enjoy fruit to satisfy sweet cravings.

### 9. Mindful Eating

Practising mindful eating involves paying attention to what and how much you eat, leading to better portion control and a more enjoyable eating experience.

- » Techniques: Eat slowly, savour each bite, and avoid distractions like TV or smartphones during meals.

### 10. Consultation with a Dietitian

Collaborating with a registered dietitian can provide personalised guidance and support tailored to your specific needs.

- » Benefits: A dietitian can help create a meal plan that suits your lifestyle, preferences, and medical needs, ensuring that you get the nutrients you need while managing your diabetes effectively.

By incorporating these core principles into your daily routine, you can take control of your diabetes and improve your overall health. The Diabetic Diet is not just about what you eat, but how you approach eating—making mindful, informed choices that support a balanced and healthy life.

## Cultural and Historical Background

In understanding the Diabetic Diet as it stands today, it is essential to appreciate its cultural and historical foundations, which have shaped its evolution into a vital component of modern diabetes management in the UK.

### Historical Context

The management of diabetes through diet has a rich history dating back centuries. In ancient times, physicians recognised theimportance of dietary restrictions in managing symptoms akin to diabetes. However, it was not until the early 20th century that groundbreaking research by scientists such as Frederick Banting and Charles Best led to the discovery of insulin, revolutionising diabetes treatment.

In the UK, the development of dietary guidelines for diabetes management evolved alongside advances in medical research and nutritional science. Early dietary recommendations focused on carbohydrate restriction and calorie control to manage blood sugar levels. Over time, the emphasis shifted towards a more balanced approach that considers the quality and timing of nutrient intake.

## Cultural Influences

Cultural influences have also played a significant role in shaping dietary practices for individuals with diabetes in the UK. Traditional British cuisine, known for its hearty dishes and use of seasonal ingredients, has adapted to include healthier options that cater to dietary restrictions.

Moreover, multiculturalism has enriched the dietary landscape, introducing a variety of cuisines that offer diverse flavours and nutritious alternatives. The integration of Mediterranean, Asian, and Middle Eastern culinary traditions, for instance, has introduced beneficial components such as olive oil, whole grains, and spices known for their health-promoting properties.

## Modern Nutritional Science

Today, the Diabetic Diet in the UK is grounded in modern nutritional science, which continues to refine our understanding of how dietary choices impact diabetes management. Research supports the benefits of a balanced diet rich in whole grains, lean proteins, healthy fats, and a variety of fruits and vegetables. These foods provide essential nutrients, antioxidants, and dietary fibre, which help regulate blood sugar levels, support cardiovascular health, and enhance overall well-being.

## Dietary Guidelines and Recommendations

The development of dietary guidelines specific to diabetes management in the UK reflects ongoing collaboration between healthcare professionals, nutritionists, and researchers. These guidelines aim to provide clear, evidence-based recommendations that empower individuals with diabetes to make informed choices about their diet.

## Cultural Sensitivity in Dietary Advice

Recognising cultural diversity is crucial in providing effective dietary advice. Healthcare providers strive to offer personalised recommendations that respect cultural preferences and traditions while promoting optimal health outcomes. This approach ensures that dietary advice is not only effective but also culturally sensitive, fostering trust and adherence among individuals with diabetes.

# Importance of Adopting the Diabetic Diet

The decision to adopt the Diabetic Diet is not merely a choice of dietary regimen but an initiative-taking step towards managing diabetes effectively and enhancing overall health and well-being. For individuals in the UK grappling with diabetes, whether Type 1 or Type 2, embracing this dietary approach can yield profound benefits that extend far beyond blood sugar control.

## Managing Blood Sugar Levels

Central to the Diabetic Diet is its ability to regulate blood sugar levels, which is crucial for diabetes management. By focusing on balanced meals that include complex carbohydrates, lean proteins, and healthy fats, individuals can achieve more stable glucose readings throughout the day. Consistent monitoring of carbohydrate intake, along with adherence to meal timing guidelines, helps to minimise fluctuations and reduce the risk of hyperglycaemia (high blood sugar) or hypoglycaemia (low blood sugar) episodes.

## Supporting Weight Management

Weight management plays a pivotal role in diabetes care, particularly for individuals with Type 2 diabetes. Excess weight can exacerbate insulin resistance, making blood sugar control more challenging. The Diabetic Diet encourages portion control, emphasises nutrient-dense foods, and discourages the consumption of sugary and processed foods. These dietary strategies not only aid in weight loss but also promote the maintenance of a healthy body weight, which is essential for long-term diabetes management and overall health.

## Enhancing Cardiovascular Health

Diabetes is often associated with an increased risk of cardiovascular diseases, including heart attack and stroke. Adopting the Diabetic Diet, which prioritises heart-healthy fats (such as those found in fish, nuts, and olive oil), whole grains, and fibre-rich fruits and vegetables, can help manage cholesterol levels, lower blood pressure, and reduce the risk of cardiovascular complications. These dietary choices contribute to improved heart health and overall cardiovascular well-being.

## Improving Energy Levels and Quality of Life

A balanced Diabetic Diet provides the necessary nutrients and energy to sustain daily activities while minimising the impact of blood sugar fluctuations. By consuming regular meals and snacks that are rich in complex carbohydrates and proteins, individuals with diabetes can experience sustained energy levels throughout the day. This steady energy supply supports overall vitality and enhances quality of life, allowing for greater engagement in daily pursuits and activities.

## Preventing Long-Term Complications

Consistent adherence to the Diabetic Diet can help mitigate the risk of long-term complications associated with diabetes. These may include nerve damage (neuropathy), kidney disease (nephropathy), eye damage (retinopathy), and foot problems. By maintaining optimal blood sugar control through dietary management, individuals can significantly reduce their likelihood of developing these serious complications and preserve their long-term health.

### Promoting a Holistic Approach to Health

Beyond dietary considerations, the Diabetic Diet promotes an integrated approach to health that encompasses physical activity, stress management, and adequate sleep. Regular physical activity, in combination with a balanced diet, helps control weight, improve insulin sensitivity, and enhance cardiovascular fitness. Stress management techniques, such as mindfulness and relaxation exercises, contribute to better blood sugar control and overall well-being. Adequate sleep supports metabolic function and hormone regulation, further supporting diabetes management efforts.

### Tailoring to Individual Needs

One of the strengths of the Diabetic Diet lies in its adaptability to individual preferences, cultural backgrounds, and medical conditions. Collaborating closely with a registered dietitian allows for personalised dietary guidance that considers specific health goals, food preferences, and lifestyle factors. This tailored approach ensures that dietary recommendations are practical, sustainable, and effective in managing diabetes while supporting overall health and well-being.

## Encouragement and Motivation

Navigating life with diabetes presents unique challenges that require perseverance, resilience, and an initiative-taking approach to health. This subchapter aims to provide encouragement and motivation for individuals who are embarking on or continuing their journey with diabetes management through the Diabetic Diet.

### Understanding the Journey

Managing diabetes is a journey that demands commitment and dedication. It involves making daily choices that impact your health and well-being. While there may be moments of frustration or setbacks, it is important to remember that every small step towards better health matters.

### Celebrating Progress

Celebrate your successes, no matter how small they may seem. Whether it is achieving stable blood sugar levels, adopting healthier eating habits, or incorporating regular physical activity into your routine, each achievement contributes to your overall well-being.

### Setting Realistic Goals

Set realistic and achievable goals that align with your personal health objectives. Whether your focus is on improving your diet, increasing physical activity, or managing stress, breaking down larger goals into smaller, manageable steps can make them more attainable.

## Embracing Support Networks

Seek support from family, friends, healthcare professionals, and the diabetes community. Sharing experiences, challenges, and successes with others who understand can provide valuable encouragement and motivation. Support groups, both online and in person, offer opportunities to connect with peers facing similar experiences.

## Staying Informed

Stay informed about advancements in diabetes management, nutrition, and lifestyle strategies. Knowledge empowers you to make informed decisions about your health and enhances your ability to manage diabetes effectively. Regularly consult reliable sources of information and stay engaged in ongoing learning.

## Cultivating Positive Habits

Develop positive habits that support your overall health and well-being. Incorporate nutritious foods into your diet, practice regular physical activity that you enjoy, prioritise adequate sleep, and manage stress through relaxation techniques or hobbies that bring you joy.

## Fostering Resilience

Build resilience to navigate challenges effectively. Recognise that setbacks are a natural part of any journey and view them as opportunities to gain experience and adjust your approach. Maintain a positive mindset, focus on your strengths, and seek out solutions when faced with obstacles.

## Monitoring Progress

Regularly monitor your blood sugar levels and other health metrics to track your progress. Use this information to make informed adjustments to your diet, exercise routine, or medication regimen as needed. Celebrate improvements and use setbacks as opportunities for reflection and growth.

## Seeking Professional Guidance

Consult with healthcare professionals, including doctors, dietitians, and diabetes educators, who specialise in diabetes management. They can provide personalised guidance, answer your questions, and offer support tailored to your individual needs and circumstances.

# 1 - GETTING STARTED

## Kitchen Essentials - Must-have Tools and Appliances

Creating a kitchen environment equipped with the right tools and appliances is crucial for anyone managing diabetes. Properly outfitted, your kitchen can help you efficiently prepare healthy meals that adhere to diabetic dietary guidelines. Below, we will explore the essential items that will make your cooking experience both enjoyable and health-promoting.

### Essential Tools

1. Digital Kitchen Scale: Precise portion control is fundamental in diabetes management, particularly when it comes to carbohydrates. A digital kitchen scale allows you to measure food portions accurately, ensuring you stay within your recommended intake.
2. Measuring Cups and Spoons: These are vital for gauging the correct amounts of liquids, dry ingredients, and fats. Accurate measurements help maintain portion control and consistency, which are key in managing blood glucose levels.
3. Sharp Knives: A set of high-quality, sharp knives can make food preparation safer and more efficient. Essential knives include a chef's knife for routine use, a paring knife for small tasks, and a serrated knife for cutting bread and soft vegetables.
4. Cutting Boards: To prevent cross-contamination, have separate cutting boards for raw meats and for fruits and vegetables. Opt for non-porous materials like plastic or glass, which are easier to sanitise than wooden boards.
5. Vegetable Peeler: A sturdy vegetable peeler is essential for easily preparing a variety of vegetables, which are a cornerstone of a diabetic-friendly diet.
6. Can Opener: A reliable can opener is necessary for opening canned goods like beans, tomatoes, and fish, which can be staples in many healthy recipes.
7. Mixing Bowls: A set of mixing bowls in diverse sizes is useful for combining ingredients, marinating meats, and tossing salads. Choose bowls made of stainless steel or glass for durability and ease of cleaning.
8. Whisk and Spatula: A whisk is ideal for mixing ingredients smoothly, while a spatula is perfect for scraping bowls and pans clean without damaging non-stick surfaces.
9. Colander: Essential for draining pasta, rinsing vegetables, and washing fruits, a colander should be durable and easy to clean.
10. Food Storage Containers: Invest in a variety of airtight containers to store leftovers, pre-prepared meals, and pantry staples. This helps maintain freshness and prevent food waste.

### Must-have Appliances

1. 1. Quality Blender: A versatile blender is useful for preparing smoothies, soups, and sauces using fresh, whole ingredients. Look for one with variable speeds and a durable, easy-to-clean design.

2. Food Processor: A food processor can significantly speed up the preparation process by chopping, slicing, and grating vegetables, nuts, and fruits. This appliance is invaluable for making nutrient-dense dishes quickly.
3. Slow Cooker or Crock-Pot: Perfect for preparing hearty stews, soups, and tender meats with minimal effort. A slow cooker allows ingredients to simmer slowly, enhancing flavours while you focus on other tasks.
4. Non-stick Frying Pan and Saucepan: Invest in high-quality non-stick cookware to reduce the need for excess oils and fats, promoting heart health and aiding weight management.
5. Toaster or Toaster Oven: Useful for toasting whole grain bread, warming up leftovers, or quickly preparing open-faced sandwiches and snacks.
6. Oven Thermometer: Ensuring your oven is accurately calibrated is crucial for baking and roasting foods at the correct temperatures, which is essential for achieving consistent cooking results.
7. Electric Kettle: A quick and energy-efficient way to boil water for tea, coffee, or cooking purposes without using the stovetop.

Equipping your kitchen with these essential tools and appliances sets a solid foundation for effective diabetes management through nutritious meal preparation. These items enhance kitchen efficiency, ensure safety, and empower you to enjoy cooking while prioritising your health. By investing in quality kitchen essentials, you pave the way for a successful journey towards better health and well-being in managing diabetes.

## Pantry Basics - Stocking Diabetic-friendly Ingredients

Creating a well-stocked pantry is a crucial step in managing diabetes effectively. Having a variety of healthy, diabetes-friendly ingredients on hand ensures that you can prepare nutritious meals and snacks with ease. This subchapter will guide you through the essentials of stocking a pantry that supports your dietary needs and helps you maintain stable blood sugar levels.

### Whole Grains

- » Quinoa: A versatile grain that is high in protein and fibre, quinoa can be used in salads, as a side dish, or in place of rice.
- » Brown Rice: This whole grain is a major source of fibre and provides sustained energy. Use it as a base for stir-fries, curries, and bowls.
- » Whole Grain Pasta: Opt for whole grain or legume-based pasta for a higher fibre and protein content, helping to manage blood sugar spikes.
- » Oats: A pantry staple, oats are perfect for a hearty breakfast, adding to smoothies, or baking into healthy snacks.

### Legumes and Beans

- » Lentils: Packed with protein and fibre, lentils are excellent for soups, stews, and salads.
- » Chickpeas: Versatile and nutritious, chickpeas can be used in hummus, roasted for snacks, or added to salads and stews.

- Black Beans: These beans are rich in protein and fibre, making them ideal for soups, casseroles, and Mexican-inspired dishes.
- Kidney Beans: Great for chilli, salads, and stews, kidney beans add both texture and nutrition to your meals.

## Nuts and Seeds

- Almonds: A great snack option that provides healthy fats, protein, and fibre. Use them in salads, baking, or as a quick snack.
- Chia Seeds: These tiny seeds are rich in omega-3 fatty acids, fibre, and protein. They can be used in puddings, smoothies, and baking.
- Flaxseeds: Ground flaxseeds are a useful source of omega-3s and fibre. Add them to smoothies, oatmeal, or baking recipes.
- Pumpkin Seeds: High in magnesium and healthy fats, pumpkin seeds are perfect for adding crunch to salads or eating as a snack.

## Healthy Oils and Fats

- Olive Oil: Extra virgin olive oil is a staple for cooking and dressings, providing heart-healthy monounsaturated fats.
- Coconut Oil: While higher in saturated fat, coconut oil can be used in moderation for baking and cooking.
- Avocado Oil: Ideal for high-heat cooking, avocado oil is rich in monounsaturated fats and has a mild flavour.
- Nut Butters: Natural nut butters (without added sugar) like almond or peanut butter are great for snacks and adding to smoothies or toast.

## Low-Glycaemic Index Carbohydrates

- Sweet Potatoes: These are lower on the glycaemic index and rich in vitamins and fibre. Use them in baking, mashes, or as fries.
- Whole Wheat Bread: Choose whole wheat or whole grain bread to increase fibre intake and reduce blood sugar spikes.
- Bulgar Wheat: A low-GI grain that is perfect for salads and side dishes, providing a steady release of energy.
- Barley: Another low-GI grain, barley is excellent in soups, stews, and salads.

## Herbs and Spices

- Cinnamon: This spice can help manage blood sugar levels and adds flavour to both sweet and savoury dishes.
- Turmeric: Known for its anti-inflammatory properties, turmeric can be used in curries, soups, and smoothies.

- » Garlic: Fresh garlic adds flavour and has potential blood sugar-lowering properties.
- » Basil, Oregano, Thyme: Fresh or dried herbs can enhance the flavour of dishes without adding extra calories or sodium.

## **Canned and Jarred Goods**

- » Tomatoes: Canned tomatoes (without added sugar) are versatile for sauces, soups, and stews.
- » Tuna: Canned tuna in water is a convenient source of protein for salads, sandwiches, and casseroles.
- » Olives: Rich in healthy fats, olives can be added to salads, pasta dishes, or eaten as a snack.
- » Artichoke Hearts: These are great in salads and pasta dishes, adding flavour and fibre.

## **Fresh Produce**

- » Leafy Greens: Spinach, kale, and Swiss chard are nutrient-dense and can be used in salads, smoothies, and cooking.
- » Berries: Blueberries, strawberries, and raspberries are low in sugar and high in antioxidants, perfect for snacks or adding to yogurt and oatmeal.
- » Cruciferous Vegetables: Broccoli, cauliflower, and Brussels sprouts are high in fibre and essential nutrients, ideal for roasting, steaming, or adding to stir-fries.
- » Citrus Fruits: Oranges, lemons, and limes are rich in vitamin C and can enhance the flavour of dishes and beverages.

## **Dairy and Dairy Alternatives**

- » Greek Yogurt: High in protein and lower in carbohydrates, Greek yogurt can be used in -smoothies, as a snack, or in cooking.
- » Milk Alternatives: Unsweetened almond milk, soy milk, and oat milk are good alternatives for those who are lactose intolerant or prefer plant-based options.
- » Cheese: Hard cheeses like cheddar and Parmesan, in moderation, provide protein and flavour to meals and snacks.
- » Cottage Cheese: Low in fat and high in protein, cottage cheese is a versatile addition to breakfasts and snacks.

Stocking your pantry with these diabetic-friendly ingredients sets the stage for preparing healthy, balanced meals that support blood sugar management. By having a variety of whole grains, legumes, nuts, seeds, healthy oils, low-GI carbohydrates, herbs, spices, canned goods, fresh produce, and dairy alternatives, you are well-equipped to create delicious and nutritious dishes. These pantry basics will help you make informed dietary choices, simplify meal preparation, and ensure you are always ready to enjoy a healthy, diabetes-friendly diet in the UK.

# Reading Labels - Understanding Nutritional Information

Understanding nutritional labels is an essential skill for anyone managing diabetes. It empowers you to make informed choices about the foods you consume, helping you maintain stable blood sugar levels and overall health. This subchapter will guide you through the key components of nutritional labels, providing specific tips for identifying diabetic-friendly options.

## **The Basics of Nutritional Labels**

In the UK, food labels must include certain information to help consumers make healthier choices. Here is a breakdown of the key elements:

1. Serving Size: This indicates the quantity of food that the nutritional information pertains to. It is crucial to compare this to the amount you actually eat. For example, if a serving size is 30g but you consume 60g, you will need to double the nutritional values provided. Always adjust calculations to your actual intake.
2. Calories: This measures the energy you get from a serving of the food. Managing calorie intake is important for maintaining a healthy weight, which can impact blood sugar control. For instance, a typical adult needs about 2000-2500 calories per day. Understanding your personal caloric needs can help you manage your intake appropriately.
3. Total Carbohydrates: This is one of the most critical elements for diabetics. It includes all sugars, starches, and fibre in the food. Carbohydrates directly affect blood sugar levels, so it is important to monitor their intake. The general recommendation for most people with diabetes is 45-60 grams of carbohydrates per meal, but this can vary based on individual needs and activity levels. Example: If a label states 30g of total carbohydrates per serving and you plan to have two servings, you are consuming 60g of carbohydrates. Knowing this helps you balance the rest of your meal accordingly.
4. Sugars: This includes both naturally occurring sugars and added sugars. It is important to limit added sugars as they can cause rapid spikes in blood sugar levels. The NHS recommends that adults should have no more than 30g of free sugars a day. Look for products with less than 5g of total sugar per 100g to keep sugar intake in check. Example: If a product contains 12g of sugars per serving and you eat two servings, you are consuming 24g of sugar, which is almost your entire daily recommended limit.
5. Dietary Fibre: Fibre helps slow the absorption of sugar, aiding in blood sugar control. Foods high in fibre can help keep you feeling full longer and support digestive health. Aim for at least 30g of fibre per day. Foods are considered high in fibre if they contain more than 6g per 100g. Example: If a food item has 8g of fibre per serving and you consume it three times a day, that's already 24g of fibre, close to your daily target.
6. Protein: Protein has negligible effect on blood sugar levels and can help you feel satisfied. It is important to include adequate protein in your diet, aiming for lean sources like chicken, fish, legumes, and tofu. Adults are recommended to consume 50-60g of protein per day. Example: If a label states 15g of protein per serving and you consume three servings of that product daily, you aregetting 45g of protein, which is beneficial for maintaining muscle mass and satiety.

7. Fats: Look for total fat, saturated fat, and trans fat information. Opt for foods with healthier fats, such as monounsaturated and polyunsaturated fats, and limit saturated and trans fats which can impact heart health. The NHS suggests that the average person should have no more than 30g of saturated fat a day, and the average woman no more than 20g a day. Example: If a product has 10g of total fat, with 2g saturated fat per serving, having three servings means you are consuming 30g of fat with 6g of saturated fat, which is a sizeable portion of your daily limit.
8. Salt (Sodium): High sodium intake can lead to high blood pressure, which is a concern for diabetics. Aim to keep your sodium intake below 6g per day. Foods with more than 1.5g salt per 100g are considered high. Example: If a food item contains 1g of salt per serving and you consume four servings, that's 4g of salt, nearing the recommended daily limit.

**Traffic Light Labelling**

In the UK, many food products use the traffic light labelling system on the front of the pack, which provides a quick visual guide to the nutritional quality of the food. Here is how to interpret it:

» Green: Indicates low levels of fat, saturated fat, sugars, and salt. These are the healthiest options.
» Amber: Indicates medium levels. These are fine to consume in moderation.
» Red: Indicates high levels. It is best to limit these foods, especially if you are managing diabetes.

**Practical Tips for Reading Labels**

» Compare Labels: When choosing between products, compare the nutritional labels to find the option with the lower carbohydrate, sugar, and sodium content and higher fibre content. For example, compare two bread brands to choose one with higher fibre and lower sugar content.
» Check Ingredient Lists: Ingredients are listed in descending order by weight. Be cautious of products where sugar or unhealthy fats are among the first few ingredients. For instance, if sugar is listed first or second, the product is high in added sugars.
» Look for Whole Foods: Opt for products with minimal ingredients and avoid those with long lists of unfamiliar ingredients, as these are often more processed and less nutritious. Whole grains, fresh produce, and lean proteins should be staples.
» Beware of "Sugar-Free" Claims: Foods labelled as "sugar-free" might still contain carbohydrates or unhealthy sugar substitutes. Always check the total carbohydrate content. For example, a sugar-free biscuit might still have prominent levels of starches that can affect blood sugar.
» Portion Awareness: Be mindful of the portion size listed on the label. It is easy to consume more than the suggested serving size, which can lead to higher intake of carbohydrates and calories. Measure your portions to stay within recommended limits.

- » Understand Different Carbohydrates: Not all carbs are created equal. Prioritise complex carbohydrates found in whole grains and vegetables over simple carbs found in processed foods and sugary snacks. Complex carbs provide more sustained energy and fibre.
- » Identify Hidden Sugars: Sugars can be listed under various names such as dextrose, fructose, maltose, and more. Familiarise yourself with these terms to avoid hidden sugars Products with less than 5g of sugars per 100g are considered low in sugar.
- » Focus on Fibre: High-fibre foods are beneficial for blood sugar control. Choose products with at least 3g of fibre per serving whenever possible. Foods like beans, lentils, and whole grains are excellent sources.

Mastering the skill of reading nutritional labels is vital for managing diabetes effectively. By understanding the information provided on food labels and making informed choices, you can better control your blood sugar levels, manage your weight, and improve your overall health. Remember to compare products, focus on whole foods, and be aware of portion sizes. With these tools at your disposal, you will be well-equipped to navigate the supermarket aisles and make healthier choices for your diabetic diet in the UK.

## 30 Food that must be banned or limited for Diabetics

When managing diabetes, certain ingredients can have a detrimental impact on blood sugar control and overall health. Here is a concise list of 30 ingredients that should be avoided or limited to help maintain stable blood sugar levels:

1. Refined Sugar: Found in sweets, baked goods, and many processed foods.
2. High-Fructose Corn Syrup: Commonly added to soft drinks and packaged foods.
3. White Flour: Used in bread, pastries, and many other baked goods.
4. White Rice: Lacks fibre and can cause blood sugar spikes.
5. Regular Pasta: Made from refined flour, leading to quick blood sugar increases.
6. Potatoes: High glycaemic index, especially when mashed or fried.
7. Sweetened Beverages: Such as regular soft drinks, sweetened teas, and flavoured waters.
8. Fruit Juices: Even 100% juice can be high in sugar without the fibre.
9. Candy: High in sugar and low in nutrients.
10. Pastries: Such as donuts, croissants, and muffins, made with refined flour and sugar.
11. Cakes: Typically, high in sugar and refined carbohydrates.
12. Ice Cream: Contains excessive amounts of sugar and fat.
13. Milk & White Chocolate: High in sugar and fat compared to dark chocolate.
14. Sugary Cereals: Many breakfast cereals have added sugars and lack fibre.
15. Canned Fruit in Syrup: Contains added sugars.
16. Jams and Jellies: Often high in added sugars.
17. Maple Syrup: High in natural sugars.
18. Honey: High in natural sugars.
19. Agave Nectar: High in fructose.
20. Ketchup: Contains added sugars.
21. Barbecue Sauce: High in sugars.

22. Sweetened Yogurt: Contains added sugars.
23. Granola Bars: Often contain added sugars and unhealthy fats.
24. Instant Noodles: High in refined carbs and sodium.
25. Microwave Popcorn: Often high in unhealthy fats and sodium.
26. Packaged Snack Cakes: High in sugars and unhealthy fats.
27. Frozen Pizza: High in refined carbs and unhealthy fats.
28. French Fries: High in unhealthy fats and carbs.
29. Processed Meats: Such as sausages and hot dogs, high in unhealthy fats and sodium.
30. Full-Fat Dairy Products: High in saturated fat, such as butter, cream, and certain cheeses.

Understanding which ingredients to avoid or limit is crucial for effective diabetes management. By focusing on whole, minimally processed foods and being mindful of ingredient labels, you can make healthier choices that support stable blood sugar levels and overall health. Consulting with a healthcare professional or dietitian can also help tailor a diet plan that meets your individual needs and preferences.

## Moving Forward

With the foundation laid in this chapter, you are now equipped to make smarter, more informed choices in your kitchen and at the supermarket. The principles and practices discussed here will serve as the backbone of your dietary management plan.

As you proceed to the subsequent chapters, you will delve deeper into specific meal planning, cooking techniques, and recipes tailored to support your diabetic journey. Remember, the goal is not only to manage your diabetes but also to enjoy a varied and delicious diet that enhances your overall wellbeing.

Your journey towards better health is a continuous process of learning and adapting. Embrace these changes with a positive mindset and the understanding that each small step brings you closer to optimal health. With the knowledge gained in this chapter, you are well on your way to mastering the art of diabetic-friendly cooking and eating, setting a solid foundation for a healthier and more balanced life.

Remember, managing diabetes through diet is not about deprivation but about making smarter, more informed choices that lead to a healthier lifestyle! With each meal, you have the power to positively impact your health. Stay motivated, keep learning, and do not hesitate to seek support from healthcare professionals, family, and friends. Together, these elements will help you thrive and maintain control over your diabetes.

# 2 - BREAKFAST BOOSTERS

## Why Breakfast Matters: Importance of a Healthy Start

Breakfast is often touted as the most important meal of the day, and for good reason, especially for individuals managing diabetes. Starting your day with a balanced, nutritious breakfast sets the tone for your blood sugar levels, energy, and overall well-being. This subchapter delves into the significance of breakfast for diabetics, offering detailed insights into how a healthy start can make a substantial difference in managing diabetes effectively.

### 1. Stabilising Blood Sugar Levels

For people with diabetes, maintaining stable blood sugar levels is crucial. After a night's fast, your blood sugar levels are likely to be lower. A well-balanced breakfast helps to kickstart your metabolism and provides a steady release of glucose into the bloodstream. This prevents the dramatic spikes and drops that can occur if you skip breakfast or consume an imbalanced meal. Example: Consuming a breakfast that includes complex carbohydrates (such as whole grains), lean proteins, and healthy fats can help ensure a gradual rise in blood sugar levels, rather than a sharp spike.

### 2. Energy Boost and Mental Clarity

Starting your day with a nutritious breakfast not only fuels your body but also your mind. A balanced breakfast helps replenish glucose levels, which is essential for brain function. This is particularly important for diabetics, as fluctuating blood sugar levels can affect cognitive functions, concentration, and mood. Example: A breakfast rich in protein and fibre, like a vegetable omelette with whole grain toast, provides sustained energy and keeps you focused throughout the morning.

### 3. Weight Management

Skipping breakfast can lead to increased hunger later in the day, which may result in overeating or choosing unhealthy snacks. This is particularly problematic for diabetics, as weight management is a critical component of diabetes control. Eating a healthy breakfast can help regulate your appetite and prevent the urge to consume high-calorie, high-sugar foods. Example: A bowl of oatmeal topped with berries and nuts can keep you full and satisfied, reducing the temptation to snack on unhealthy options before lunch.

### 4. Nutritional Intake

Breakfast is an excellent opportunity to incorporate essential nutrients into your diet. A nutritious breakfast can provide important vitamins, minerals, and other nutrients that support overall health. For diabetics, ensuring a high intake of fibre, vitamins, and minerals is particularly beneficial for managing the condition and preventing complications. Example: Greek yogurt with chia seeds and fresh fruit is a powerhouse of protein, fibre, and antioxidants, contributing to your daily nutritional needs.

## 5. Improved Insulin Sensitivity

Regularly consuming a healthy breakfast has been shown to improve insulin sensitivity. This means that your body becomes more effective at using insulin to lower blood sugar levels. Improved insulin sensitivity can help manage diabetes more effectively and reduce the risk of long-term complications. Example: Including foods like whole grains and fruits that are high in fibre can enhance insulin sensitivity and improve blood sugar control.

## Practical Tips for a Healthy Diabetic Breakfast

- Balance Your Macronutrients: Aim to include a mix of carbohydrates, proteins, and healthy fats. This balance helps regulate blood sugar and provides sustained energy. Example: A balanced breakfast could be scrambled eggs with spinach and tomatoes, a slice of whole grain toast, and a small piece of fruit.
- Choose Low-Glycaemic Index (GI) Foods: Foods with a low GI release glucose more slowly and steadily. This is beneficial for managing blood sugar levels. Example: Opt for steel-cut oats over instant oatmeal, as they have a lower GI and provide more sustained energy.
- Include Fibre-Rich Foods: Fibre slows down the absorption of sugar and can improve blood sugar control. Example: Incorporate fruits like berries, which are high in fibre and have a lower impact on blood sugar levels.
- Watch Portion Sizes: Even healthy foods can affect blood sugar levels if consumed in copious quantities. Be mindful of portion sizes to maintain optimal blood sugar control. Example: Measure out servings of cereal and avoid overfilling your bowl.
- Stay Hydrated: Starting your day with a glass of water can help with overall hydration and support metabolic processes. Example: Drinking water with a slice of lemon before eating can kickstart your metabolism and aid digestion.

## Conclusion

A healthy breakfast is a cornerstone of effective diabetes management. By prioritising a balanced, nutrient-rich breakfast, you set the stage for stable blood sugar levels, sustained energy, and overall well-being. Remember, the goal is to create a breakfast that not only satisfies your hunger but also supports your health. Incorporate these practices into your daily routine to enjoy the benefits of a well-managed diabetic diet.

# Scrambled Tofu with Vegetables

## Ingredients

- 200g firm tofu, drained and crumbled
- 1 tablespoon olive oil (15ml)
- 1 small red onion (approx. 70g), finely chopped
- 1 red bell pepper (approx. 150g), diced
- 1 medium courgette (approx. 200g), diced
- 100g fresh spinach leaves, chopped
- 2 cloves garlic, minced
- 1 teaspoon ground turmeric (5g)
- 1 teaspoon ground cumin (5g)
- 1 teaspoon paprika (5g)
- 1/2 teaspoon ground black pepper (2g)
- 1/2 teaspoon salt (2g), or to taste
- 2 tablespoons fresh parsley, chopped
- 1 tablespoon nutritional yeast (optional, 10g)

**Prep. time:** 10 min | **Total time:** 25 min | **Servings:** 2

## Directions

1. Drain the firm tofu and crumble it into small pieces with your hands or a fork. Set aside.
2. Heat the olive oil in a large non-stick frying pan over medium heat. Add the finely chopped red onion and sauté for 2-3 minutes until it starts to soften. Add the diced red bell pepper and courgette to the pan, cooking for another 5 minutes until the vegetables are tender. Add the minced garlic and cook for another 1 minute, stirring frequently to prevent burning.
3. Add the crumbled tofu to the pan with the vegetables. Sprinkle the ground turmeric, ground cumin, paprika, ground black pepper, and salt over the tofu and vegetables. Stir well to combine and cook for 5 minutes, allowing the tofu to heat through and absorb the flavours of the spices.
4. Add the chopped spinach leaves to the pan and cook for another 2 minutes until the spinach has wilted. Stir in the chopped fresh parsley and nutritional yeast (if using) just before serving.
5. Divide the scrambled tofu with vegetables between 2 plates. Garnish with a sprinkle of fresh parsley for a touch of colour and added flavour.

**Nutritional value (per serving):**

Calories - 262 kcal
Protein - 15.6g
Carbohydrates - 22.7g
Sugars - 8.1g
Fibre - 8.7g
Fat - 13.6g
Saturated Fat - 2.5

**Minimising Sugars:** Use fresh vegetables and avoid any pre-packaged options that may contain added sugars.

**Flavour Enhancements:** For extra flavour without added sodium, consider adding a pinch of smoked paprika or fresh herbs like basil or coriander.

**Gluten-Free:** This recipe is naturally gluten-free.

**Vegan:** This recipe is vegan friendly using plant-based ingredients.

# Whole Grain Toast with Smashed Avocado and Tomatoes

## Ingredients

- 2 slices whole grain bread (approx. 60g each)
- 1 large ripe avocado (approx. 200g)
- 100g cherry tomatoes, halved
- 1 tablespoon extra-virgin olive oil (15ml)
- 1 tablespoon fresh lemon juice (15ml)
- 1/2 teaspoon ground black pepper (2g)
- 1/4 teaspoon salt (1g), or to taste
- 1 teaspoon fresh parsley, chopped (optional)
- 1 teaspoon fresh basil, chopped (optional)
- 1/2 teaspoon chilli flakes (optional)

**Prep. time:** 10 min | **Total time:** 15 min | **Servings:** 2

## Directions

1. Toast the slices of whole grain bread until they are golden brown and crispy. This should take about 2-3 minutes in a toaster or under a grill.
2. Cut the avocado in half, remove the pit, and scoop the flesh into a bowl. Add the fresh lemon juice, ground black pepper, and salt to the avocado. Mash the avocado with a fork until it reaches your desired consistency (smooth or chunky).
3. Halve the cherry tomatoes and set them aside.
4. Spread the mashed avocado evenly over the toasted whole grain bread. Top each slice with halved cherry tomatoes. Drizzle with extra virgin olive oil.
5. Sprinkle fresh parsley, basil, and chilli flakes over the top for added flavour and a touch of spice (optional).
6. Serve the toast immediately while the bread is still warm, and the avocado is fresh.

---

Nutritional value (per serving):

Calories – 269.4 kcal (without optional ingredients) or 288.1 kcal (with them)
Protein – 13.8g or 16.1g
Carbohydrates – 22.5g or 24.2g
Sugars – 8.4g or 8.5g
Fibre – 7.35g or 8.7g
Fat – 13.8g or 14.1g
Saturated Fat – 2.6g

**Minimising Sugars:** Use fresh, unprocessed ingredients to avoid added sugars.

**Flavour Enhancements:** Fresh herbs like parsley and basil enhance flavour without adding extra sodium. A sprinkle of chilli flakes can add a spicy kick.

**Gluten-Free:** This recipe is naturally gluten-free.

**Vegan:** This recipe is veganfriendly using plant-based ingredients.

# Greek Yoghurt with Nuts and Fresh

### Ingredients

- 300g Greek yogurt (plain, unsweetened)
- 100g mixed fresh berries (e.g., strawberries, blueberries, raspberries)
- 30g walnuts, roughly chopped
- 1 tablespoon chia seeds (15g)
- 1 tablespoon flaxseeds (15g)
- 1 teaspoon ground cinnamon (5g)
- 1 teaspoon pure vanilla extract (5ml)
- 1 tablespoon unsweetened shredded coconut (optional, 15g)
- 1 tablespoon fresh mint leaves, chopped (optional, 15g)

**Prep. time:** 10 min | **Total time:** 10 min | **Servings:** 2

### Directions

1. Wash and pat dry the fresh berries. Roughly chop the almonds and walnuts. Chop the fresh mint leaves if using.
2. Divide the Greek yogurt evenly between two serving bowls. Add 50g of mixed fresh berries to each bowl. Sprinkle 15g of chopped almonds and 15g of chopped walnuts over the yogurt in each bowl. Add 7.5g (half tablespoon) of chia seeds and 7.5g (half tablespoon) of flaxseeds to each bowl. Sprinkle 2.5g (half teaspoon) of ground cinnamon over the top. Drizzle 2.5ml (half teaspoon) of pure vanilla extract over each serving. Optionally, sprinkle 7.5g (half tablespoon) of unsweetened shredded coconut and 7.5g (half tablespoon) of chopped fresh mint leaves over the top.
3. Gently mix the ingredients in each bowl to combine. Serve immediately while the yogurt is fresh, and the nuts are crunchy.

---

Nutritional value (per serving):

Calories – 409.9 kcal (without optional ingredients) or 454.9 kcal (with them)
Protein – 17.75g or 18.25g
Carbohydrates – 21.5g or 23.25g
Sugars – 8.9g or 9.4g
Fibre – 10.65g or 11.9g
Fat – 28.1g or 32.1g
Saturated Fat – 4.8g or 8.3g

**Minimising Sugars:** Use plain, unsweetened Greek yogurt and fresh berries to avoid added sugars. Avoid flavoured yogurts, which often contain added sugars.

**Flavour Enhancements:** Ground cinnamon and pure vanilla extract enhance flavour without adding sugar. Fresh mint leaves add a refreshing taste.

**Gluten-Free:** This recipe is naturally gluten-free.

**Vegan:** Substitute Greek yogurt with a plain, unsweetened plant-based yogurt (e.g., almond or coconut yogurt).

# Quinoa Bowl with Berries and Nuts

## Ingredients

- 100g quinoa
- 240ml water
- 1/4 teaspoon salt
- 150g mixed fresh berries (e.g., strawberries, blueberries, raspberries)
- 30g almonds, chopped
- 30g walnuts, chopped
- 2 tablespoons chia seeds (30g)
- 1 teaspoon ground cinnamon (5g)
- 1 teaspoon pure vanilla extract (5ml)
- 200ml unsweetened almond milk
- 1 tablespoon fresh mint leaves, chopped (optional, 15g)

**Prep. time:** 10 min | **Total time:** 25 min | **Servings:** 2

## Directions

1. Rinse the quinoa under cold water to remove any bitterness. In a medium saucepan, combine the quinoa, water, and salt. Bring to a boil over medium-high heat. Reduce heat to low, cover, and simmer for 15 minutes, or until the water is absorbed and the quinoa is tender. Remove from heat and let it sit, covered, for 5 minutes. Fluff with a fork.
2. Wash and pat dry the fresh berries. Roughly chop the almonds and walnuts. Chop the fresh mint leaves if using.
3. Divide the cooked quinoa evenly between two serving bowls. Add 75g of mixed fresh berries to each bowl. Sprinkle 15g of chopped almonds and 15g of chopped walnuts over the quinoa in each bowl. Add 15g (1 tablespoon) of chia seeds to each bowl. Sprinkle 2.5g (1/2 teaspoon) of ground cinnamon over each bowl. Drizzle 2.5ml (1/2 teaspoon) of pure vanilla extract over each serving. Pour 100ml of unsweetened almond milk into each bowl. Optionally, sprinkle 7.5g (1/2 tablespoon) of chopped fresh mint leaves over the top.
4. Gently mix the ingredients in each bowl to combine. Serve immediately while the quinoa is warm, and the nuts are crunchy.

---

Nutritional value (per serving):

Calories – 519.04 kcal
Protein – 15.88g
Carbohydrates – 53.85g
Sugars – 6.6g
Fibre – 15.65g
Fat – 26.68g
Saturated Fat – 2.45g

**Minimising Sugars:** Use unsweetened almond milk and fresh berries to avoid added sugars. Avoid sweetened milk alternatives and canned fruits.

**Flavour Enhancements:** Ground cinnamon and pure vanilla extract enhance flavour without adding sugar. Fresh mint leaves add a refreshing taste.

**Gluten-Free:** This recipe is naturally gluten-free.

**Vegan:** This recipe is suitable for vegans as it uses almond milk and plant-based ingredients.

# Cottage Cheese and Berry Parfait

## Ingredients

- 200g low-fat cottage cheese
- 150g mixed fresh berries (e.g., strawberries, blueberries, raspberries)
- 1 tablespoon chia seeds (15g)
- 1 teaspoon pure vanilla extract (5ml)
- 1 teaspoon ground cinnamon (5g)
- 30g almonds, chopped
- 30g walnuts, chopped
- 1 tablespoon unsweetened coconut flakes (optional, 15g)
- Fresh mint leaves for garnish (optional)

**Prep. time:** 10 min | **Total time:** 10 min | **Servings:** 2

## Directions

1. Wash and pat dry the fresh berries. Roughly chop the almonds and walnuts.
2. In two serving glasses or bowls, start by layering 50g of cottage cheese at the bottom of each glass. Add a layer of mixed berries (75g per serving) over the cottage cheese. Sprinkle 7.5g (1/2 tablespoon) of chia seeds on top of the berries in each glass. Add another layer of 50g of cottage cheese over the chia seeds in each glass. Sprinkle 2.5ml (1/2 teaspoon) of pure vanilla extract and 2.5g (1/2 teaspoon) of ground cinnamon over the top layer of cottage cheese in each glass. Top each parfait with 15g of chopped almonds and 15g of chopped walnuts.
3. If using, sprinkle 7.5g (1/2 tablespoon) of unsweetened coconut flakes over each parfait. Garnish with fresh mint leaves for an added touch of flavour and presentation.
4. Serve the Cottage Cheese and Berry Parfait immediately while the ingredients are fresh and crisp.

---

Nutritional value (per serving):

Calories – 362.62 kcal (without) or 410.72 kcal (with optional ingredients)
Protein – 20.45g or 21.05g
Carbohydrates – 20.75g or 22.95g
Sugars – 8.8g or 9.3g
Fibre – 9.75g or 11.25g
Fat – 21.98g or 26.08g
Saturated Fat – 2.58g or 6.28g

**Minimising Sugars:** Use fresh berries instead of sweetened varieties and choose low-fat cottage cheese to keep the dish light and healthy.

**Flavour Enhancements:** Ground cinnamon and pure vanilla extract add sweetness and depth of flavour without adding sugar.

**Gluten-Free:** This recipe isnaturally gluten-free.

**Vegan:** Replace cottage cheese with a plant-based yogurt alternative, such as almond or coconut yogurt.

# Vegetable Omelette with Mushrooms and Bell Peppers

## Ingredients

- 4 large eggs
- 100g mushrooms, thinly sliced
- 1 medium bell pepper (red or yellow), diced
- 1 small onion, finely chopped
- 1 garlic clove, minced
- 1 tablespoon olive oil (15ml)
- Salt and pepper to taste
- Fresh herbs (e.g., parsley or chives), finely chopped, for garnish

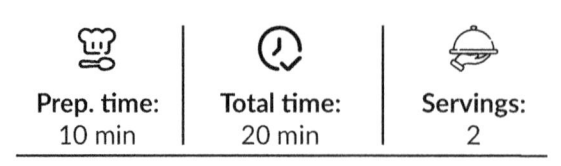

**Prep. time:** 10 min | **Total time:** 20 min | **Servings:** 2

## Directions

1. Thinly slice the mushrooms, dice the bell pepper, finely chop the onion, mince the garlic, and chop the fresh herbs for garnish.
2. Heat olive oil in a non-stick frying pan over medium heat. Add the onions and garlic, sauté for 2-3 minutes until softened. Add the mushrooms and bell pepper, cook for another 5-6 minutes until tender. Season with salt and pepper to taste. Remove from heat and set aside.
3. In a mixing bowl, whisk the eggs until well combined. Season with a pinch of salt and pepper. Heat a separate non-stick frying pan over medium heat. Pour the beaten eggs into the pan.
4. Allow the eggs to cook undisturbed for a minute or until the edges begin to set. Spoon the cooked vegetables evenly over one half of the omelette.
5. Carefully fold the other half of the omelette over the vegetables using a spatula. Cook for another 1-2 minutes until the eggs are fully set and lightly golden on both sides.
6. Slide the Vegetable Omelette onto a serving plate. Garnish with fresh chopped herbs.

---

Nutritional value (per serving):

Calories – 261.15 kcal
Protein – 14.5g
Carbohydrates – 11.75g
Sugars – 7g
Fibre – 2.65g
Fat – 17.35g
Saturated Fat – 4.1g

---

**Minimising Sugars:** Use fresh vegetables and avoid adding sauces or condiments high in sugars.

**Flavour Enhancements:** Add herbs like parsley, chives, or basil for extra flavour without added sodium or sugar.

**Gluten-Free:** This recipe is naturally gluten-free.

**Vegan:** Substitute eggs with firm tofu or chickpea flour batter for a vegan omelette alternative.

# Oatmeal with Flaxseeds and Blueberries

## Ingredients

- 100g rolled oats
- 400ml water or unsweetened almond milk
- 2 tablespoons ground flaxseeds (20g)
- 100g fresh blueberries
- 2 tablespoons chopped nuts (e.g., almonds or walnuts), optional (20g)
- Pinch of ground cinnamon, optional
- Fresh mint leaves, for garnish (optional)

**Prep. time:** 1 min
**Total time:** 10 min
**Servings:** 2

## Directions

1. In a medium saucepan, bring water or almond milk to a boil over medium-high heat. Add the rolled oats and reduce heat to medium-low. Simmer, stirring occasionally, for about 5-7 minutes until the oats are tender and the mixture thickens.
2. Stir in the ground flaxseeds during the last minute of cooking. This adds extra fibre and omega-3 fatty acids.
3. Divide the cooked oatmeal into serving bowls. Top each bowl with fresh blueberries and chopped nuts, if using.
4. Sprinkle with ground cinnamon for extra flavour, if desired. Garnish with fresh mint leaves for a refreshing touch, if desired.

Nutritional value (per serving):

Calories – 381.05 kcal (with nuts and milk)
Protein – 11.15g
Carbohydrates – 47.1g
Sugars – 6.1g
Fibre – 10.5g
Fat – 16.45g
Saturated Fat – 1.8g

**Minimising Sugars:** Ensure you use unsweetened almond milk and avoid adding any additional sweeteners.

**Gluten-Free:** Use certified gluten-free oats if necessary.

**Vegan:** Use almond milk for a vegan-friendly version.

# Smoked Salmon and Cucumber Roll-Ups

## Ingredients

- 200g smoked salmon
- 1 large cucumber (approx. 300g)
- 100g cream cheese (low-fat or dairy-free alternative)
- 1 tablespoon fresh dill, finely chopped
- 1 tablespoon fresh chives, finely chopped
- 1 teaspoon lemon zest
- 1 tablespoon lemon juice
- Freshly ground black pepper, to taste

**Prep. time:** 15 min | **Total time:** 15 min | **Servings:** 4

## Directions

1. Wash the cucumber thoroughly. Using a vegetable peeler or mandolin slicer, slice the cucumber lengthwise into thin ribbons.
2. In a small bowl, combine the cream cheese, chopped dill, chopped chives, lemon zest, and lemon juice. Mix well until smooth. Season with freshly ground black pepper to taste.
3. Lay out the cucumber ribbons on a clean surface. Spread a thin layer of the cream cheese mixture evenly over each ribbon. Place a slice of smoked salmon on top of the cream cheese layer.
4. Starting from one end, carefully roll up the cucumber ribbon, keeping the filling intact. Secure each roll-up with a toothpick if necessary.
5. Arrange the roll-ups on a serving plate. Garnish with additional fresh dill or chives if desired.

---

**Nutritional value (per serving):**

Calories – 221 kcal
Protein – 23.1g
Carbohydrates – 7.4g
Sugars – 4.2g
Fibre – 0.95g
Fat – 11g
Saturated Fat – 4.2g

**Minimising Sugars:** Use fresh ingredients and avoid any added sugars.

**Balanced Macronutrients:** This recipe offers a balanced mix of healthy fats from salmon, protein from both salmon and cream cheese, and low- glycaemic carbohydrates from cucumber.

**Gluten-Free:** Naturally, gluten- free.

**Vegan:** Substitute the smoked salmon with thinly sliced avocado or marinated tofu and use a dairy-free cream cheese alternative.

# Avocado and Spinach Smoothie

## Ingredients

- 1 ripe avocado (approx. 150g flesh)
- 100g fresh spinach leaves
- 250ml unsweetened almond milk
- 1 medium-sized cucumber (approx. 200g)
- 1 small green apple (approx. 100g)
- 1 tablespoon chia seeds (10g)
- Juice of 1 lime (approx. 30ml)
- 1 teaspoon ground flaxseeds (5g)
- 1/2 teaspoon ground cinnamon
- 2-3 ice cubes (optional)

**Prep. time:** 10 min | **Total time:** 20 min | **Servings:** 2

## Directions

1. Halve the avocado, remove the pit, and scoop the flesh into a blender. Wash and drain the spinach leaves. Peel the cucumber and chop it into chunks. Core the green apple and chop it into chunks.
2. Add the avocado, spinach, cucumber, green apple, chia seeds, lime juice, ground flaxseeds, and ground cinnamon to the blender. Pour in the unsweetened almond milk. If you prefer a colder smoothie, add the ice cubes.
3. Blend on high speed until the mixture is smooth and creamy. If the smoothie is too thick, add a little more almond milk to reach your desired consistency.
4. Pour the smoothie into two glasses. Optionally, garnish with a sprinkle of ground cinnamon or a few chia seeds on top.

Nutritional value (per serving):

Calories – 252.9 kcal
Protein – 5.85g
Carbohydrates – 23.4g
Sugars – 7.55g
Fibre – 10.85g
Fat – 15.1g
Saturated Fat – 1.9g

**Minimising Sugars:** Use a small green apple for a less sweet option and to keep the glycaemic index low.

**Flavour Enhancements:** For extra flavour without adding sugar or sodium, consider adding fresh herbs like mint or a pinch of nutmeg.

**Gluten-Free:** Naturally, gluten-free.

**Vegan:** This recipe is vegan-friendly using unsweetened almond milk.

# Chia Seed Breakfast Bowl

## Ingredients

- 60g chia seeds
- 400ml unsweetened almond milk
- 1 teaspoon vanilla extract
- 1 tablespoon ground flaxseeds (10g)
- 100g fresh mixed berries (e.g., strawberries, blueberries, raspberries)
- 1 small apple (approx. 100g), finely chopped
- 1 tablespoon chopped walnuts (10g)
- 1 tablespoon pumpkin seeds (10g)
- 1/2 teaspoon ground cinnamon
- 1 teaspoon unsweetened cocoa powder (optional, for a chocolate twist)
- Stevia or another approved sweetener to taste (optional)

**Prep. time:** 10 min | **Total time:** 4h 10 min | **Servings:** 2

## Directions

1. In a medium bowl, combine the chia seeds, unsweetened almond milk, and vanilla extract. Stir well to ensure the chia seeds are evenly distributed and not clumped together.
2. Cover the bowl and refrigerate overnight, or for at least 4 hours, to allow the chia seeds to absorb the liquid and form a gel-like consistency.
3. Wash and dry the fresh berries. Finely chop the apple. Measure out the ground flaxseeds, chopped walnuts, and pumpkin seeds.
4. Once the chia pudding has set, give it a good stir. Divide the chia pudding evenly into two bowls. Top each bowl with half of the fresh berries, chopped apple, ground flaxseeds, chopped walnuts, and pumpkin seeds. Sprinkle ground cinnamon over the top.
5. If you are adding a chocolate twist, lightly dust with unsweetened cocoa powder. Sweeten with stevia or another approved sweetener, if desired.

---

Nutritional value (per serving):

Calories – 341.3 kcal (348 kcal with cocoa powder)
Protein – 11.2g or 11.6g
Carbohydrates – 29.8g or 30.4g
Sugars – 8.6g
Fibre – 17.8g or 18.3g
Fat – 19.7g or 20g
Saturated Fat – 2.2g or 2.35g

---

**Minimising Sugars:** Use a small amount of stevia or another approved sweetener to keep the glycaemic index low.

**Flavour Enhancements:** For extra flavour without added sugar, try adding a pinch of nutmeg or a splash of lemon juice.

**Gluten-Free:** Naturally, gluten-free.

**Vegan:** This recipe is vegan-friendly using unsweetened almond milk.

# CHAPTER 3 - WHOLESOME LUNCHES

## Balancing Macronutrients: Protein, Carbs, and Fats

Eating a balanced lunch is essential for maintaining stable blood glucose levels, providing sustained energy, and supporting overall health. For individuals with diabetes, understanding how to balance macronutrients—proteins, carbohydrates, and fats—is crucial. Each macronutrient plays a unique role in the body, and their careful integration into meals can help manage blood sugar levels and prevent spikes and dips that affect energy and wellbeing.

## **Understanding Macronutrients**

1. Proteins

Proteins are the building blocks of the body, vital for repairing tissues, producing enzymes and hormones, and supporting immune function. For diabetics, proteins are particularly beneficial as they help to stabilise blood sugar levels by slowing down the digestion of carbohydrates. This slower digestion helps prevent rapid spikes in blood glucose.

Sources of Protein:

- Lean meats: Chicken, turkey, and lean cuts of beef or pork.
- Fish: Salmon, mackerel, and sardines, which are also rich in omega-3 fatty acids.
- Plant-based proteins: Lentils, beans, chickpeas, tofu, and tempeh.
- Dairy: Greek yoghurt, cottage cheese, and low-fat cheese.
- Nuts and seeds: Almonds, walnuts, chia seeds, and flaxseeds.

2. Carbohydrates

Carbohydrates are the primary source of energy for the body, but they have the most significant impact on blood glucose levels. It is essential to choose carbohydrates with a low glycaemic index (GI) to ensure a slow and steady release of glucose into the bloodstream. High-fibre carbohydrates are especially important for diabetics as they help improve blood sugar control.

Sources of Low-GI Carbohydrates:

- Whole grains: Quinoa, brown rice, barley, and oats.
- Vegetables: Leafy greens, broccoli, cauliflower, bell peppers, and tomatoes.
- Fruits: Berries, apples, pears, and citrus fruits.
- Legumes: Lentils, chickpeas, and black beans.

3. Fats

Fats are necessary for absorbing fat-soluble vitamins (A, D, E, and K), protecting organs, and providing long-lasting energy. For diabetics, the focus should be on healthy fats that support heart health and do not contribute to insulin resistance.

Sources of Healthy Fats:

- Avocados
- Nuts and seeds
- Olive oil and other plant-based oils
- Fatty fish, like salmon and mackerel

## **Crafting a Balanced Lunch**

To create a wholesome lunch that balances these macronutrients, follow these guidelines:

1. Start with a Protein Base:

Begin your meal planning with a source of lean protein. For instance, grilled chicken, tofu, or a mix of beans and lentils can serve as the cornerstone of your lunch.

2. Incorporate Whole Grains or Vegetables:

Add a serving of whole grains or a generous portion of low-GI vegetables. Quinoa, brown rice, or a salad with a variety of colourful vegetables can provide the necessary carbohydrates.

3. Include Healthy Fats:

Enhance your meal with a source of healthy fats. A drizzle of olive oil over your salad, a serving of avocado, or a handful of nuts can complete the dish.

## **Tips for Meal Planning and Portion Control**

Portion Sizes: Use a plate method to visualise balanced meals. Half of the plate should be filled with non-starchy vegetables, a quarter with lean protein, and the remaining quarter with whole grains or starchy vegetables.

Preparation: Prepare ingredients in bulk to save time and ensure you have healthy options available throughout the week. Cook grains and proteins ahead of time and store them in portion-sized containers.

Carbohydrate Counting: Keep track of the carbohydrate content of your meals to maintain control over your blood glucose levels. Apps and food diaries can be helpful tools for this.

Balancing macronutrients at lunch is vital for managing diabetes effectively. By incorporating a mix of proteins, low-GI carbohydrates, and healthy fats into your meals, you can enjoy delicious, satisfying lunches that support stable blood sugar levels and overall health. Remember, the key to successful diabetic meal planning is variety and balance, making each meal a nutritious and enjoyable experience.

# Grilled Chicken Salad with Mixed Greens and Vinaigrette

**Prep. time:** 15 min | **Total time:** 30 min | **Servings:** 2

## Ingredients

**For the Salad:**
- 200g skinless chicken breast
- 100g mixed greens (spinach, rocket, and kale)
- 1 medium cucumber (150g), sliced
- 100g cherry tomatoes, halved
- 1 medium red bell pepper (150g), sliced
- 30g red onion, thinly sliced
- 1 medium avocado (150g), sliced

**For the Lemon Vinaigrette:**
- 2 tablespoons (30ml) extra virgin olive oil
- 1 tablespoon (15ml) freshly squeezed lemon juice
- 1 teaspoon (5ml) Dijon mustard
- 1 clove garlic, minced
- Freshly ground black pepper, to taste
- Pinch of salt (optional)

## Directions

1. Preheat your grill or grill pan to medium-high heat. Season the chicken breast with freshly ground black pepper and a pinch of salt (if using). Grill the chicken for 6-7 minutes on each side, or until it is cooked through and has an internal temperature of 75°C. Remove from the grill and let it rest for 5 minutes before slicing it into thin strips.
2. While the chicken is grilling, prepare the mixed greens, cucumber, cherry tomatoes, red bell pepper, and red onion. Combine them in a large salad bowl. Add the sliced avocado to the salad just before serving to prevent it from browning.
3. In a small bowl or jar, whisk together the olive oil, lemon juice, Dijon mustard, minced garlic, and freshly ground black pepper. Adjust seasoning to taste. If using a jar, you can shake the ingredients together until well combined.
4. Add the grilled chicken strips to the salad bowl with the mixed greens and vegetables. Drizzle the lemon vinaigrette over the salad and toss gently to combine.

## Nutritional value (per serving):

Calories – 518.8 kcal
Protein – 35.5g
Carbohydrates – 19.5g
Sugars – 6.5g
Fibre – 8.6g
Fat – 33.2g
Saturated Fat – 4.5g

**Minimising Sugars:** Use fresh, whole vegetables rather than canned or processed ones. Avoid adding sugary dressings or toppings.

**Enhancing Flavour:** Incorporate fresh herbs such as parsley, basil, or coriander for added flavour. Use spices like black pepper, paprika, or cumin to season the chicken.

**Gluten-Free:** Ensure all ingredients are gluten-free. Most elements in this recipe are naturally gluten-free.

**Vegan:** Substitute the chicken with grilled tofu or chickpeas for a plant-based protein option.

# Quinoa and Black Bean Salad with Lime dressing

## Ingredients

**For the Salad:**
- 100g quinoa
- 240ml water
- 200g black beans, drained and
- rinsed
- 1 small red bell pepper (100g),
- diced
- 1 small yellow bell pepper
- (100g), diced
- 1 small red onion (50g), finely
- chopped
- 100g cherry tomatoes, halved
- 1 small avocado (150g), diced
- 2 tablespoons (8g) fresh
- coriander, chopped

**For the Lime Dressing:**
- 2 tablespoons (30ml) extra
- virgin olive oil
- 2 tablespoons (30ml) fresh
- lime juice
- 1 teaspoon (5ml) Dijon
- mustard
- 1 clove garlic, minced
- Freshly ground black pepper,
- to taste
- Pinch of salt (optional)

**Prep. time:** 15 min | **Total time:** 30 min | **Servings:** 2

## Directions

1. Rinse the quinoa under cold water to remove any bitterness. In a medium saucepan, combine the quinoa and water. Bring to a boil over medium-high heat. Once boiling, reduce the heat to low, cover, and simmer for about 15 minutes, or until the quinoa is cooked and water is absorbed. Fluff the quinoa with a fork and let it cool slightly.
2. While the quinoa is cooking, prepare the black beans, bell peppers, red onion, cherry tomatoes, and avocado. In a large bowl, combine the cooked quinoa, black beans, bell peppers, red onion, cherry tomatoes, and avocado. Add the chopped fresh coriander.
3. In a small bowl or jar, whisk together the olive oil, lime juice, Dijon mustard, minced garlic, freshly ground black pepper, and salt (if using). If using a jar, shake the ingredients together until well combined.
4. Pour the lime dressing over the quinoa and vegetable mixture. Toss gently to combine all ingredients evenly.

---

**Nutritional value (per serving):**

Calories – 501.9 kcal
Protein – 15.6g
Carbohydrates – 49.8g
Sugars – 7.3g
Fibre – 17.6g
Fat – 26.7g
Saturated Fat – 3.6g

**Minimising Sugars:** Use fresh, whole vegetables rather than canned or processed ones. Avoid adding sugary dressings or toppings.

**Enhancing Flavour:** Incorporate fresh herbs such as parsley, basil, or coriander for added flavour. Use spices like black pepper, paprika, or cumin to season the chicken. Gluten-Free: This recipe is naturally gluten-free.

**Vegan:** This recipe is suitable for vegans as it contains no animal products.

# Turkey and Avocado Lettuce Wraps

## Ingredients

- 200g cooked turkey breast, thinly sliced or shredded
- 1 ripe avocado (approximately 150g), sliced
- 8 large lettuce leaves (e.g., Romaine or Iceberg)
- 1 medium tomato (approximately 100g), diced
- 1 small red onion (approximately 50g), thinly sliced
- 1 small cucumber (approximately 100g), julienned
- 2 tablespoons (8g) fresh coriander, chopped
- 1 tablespoon (15ml) fresh lime juice
- 1 tablespoon (15ml) extra virgin olive oil
- Freshly ground black pepper, to taste
- Pinch of salt (optional)

**Prep. time:** 10 min | **Total time:** 10 min | **Servings:** 2

## Directions

1. Thinly slice or shred the cooked turkey breast. Slice the avocado and dice the tomato. Thinly slice the red onion and julienne the cucumber. Wash and dry the lettuce leaves. Chop the fresh coriander.
2. In a small bowl, whisk together the fresh lime juice, extra virgin olive oil, freshly ground black pepper, and a pinch of salt (if using).
3. Lay the lettuce leaves flat on a clean surface. Evenly distribute the sliced turkey, avocado, tomato, red onion, cucumber, and coriander onto each lettuce leaf. Drizzle the lime dressing over the top of each wrap.
4. Gently fold the sides of the lettuce leaves over the fillings and roll up to enclose the ingredients. Secure with a toothpick if necessary and serve immediately.

---

Nutritional value (per serving):

Calories – 361.6 kcal
Protein – 33.2g
Carbohydrates – 14g
Sugars – 3.9g
Fibre – 7g
Fat – 19.2g
Saturated Fat – 2.8g

---

**Minimising Sugars:** Use fresh, whole ingredients and avoid pre-packaged or processed options. Ensure the turkey breast is not processed and does not contain added sugars or preservatives.

**Enhancing Flavour:** Add a sprinkle of paprika or a dash of chilli flakes for a bit of heat.
Incorporate herbs like parsley or basil for additional flavour without extra sodium.

**Gluten-Free:** This recipe is naturally gluten-free.

**Vegan:** Substitute the turkey with a plant-based protein such as marinated tofu or tempeh slices.

# Lentil and Vegetable Soup

## Ingredients

- 100g dried lentils
- 1 tablespoon (15ml) extra virgin olive oil
- 1 medium onion (approximately 100g), finely chopped
- 2 cloves garlic, minced
- 1 medium carrot (approximately 70g), diced
- 1 medium courgette (approximately 150g), diced
- 1 medium red bell pepper (approximately 150g), diced
- 400ml low-sodium vegetable stock
- 400g chopped tomatoes (canned, no added sugar)
- 1 teaspoon dried thyme
- 1 teaspoon dried oregano
- 1 teaspoon ground cumin
- Freshly ground black pepper, to taste
- Fresh parsley (optional), for garnish

**Prep. time:** 15 min
**Total time:** 45 min
**Servings:** 2

## Directions

1. Rinse the lentils under cold water and set aside. Finely chop the onion, mince the garlic, and dice the carrot, courgette, and red bell pepper.
2. In a large pot, heat the olive oil over medium heat. Add the chopped onion and garlic, and sauté for 3-4 minutes until the onion is translucent. Add the diced carrot, courgette, and red bell pepper. Sauté for another 5 minutes until the vegetables begin to soften.
3. Add the rinsed lentils to the pot, stirring to combine with the vegetables. Pour in the vegetable stock and chopped tomatoes and stir well. Add the dried thyme, dried oregano, ground cumin, and freshly ground black pepper. Bring the mixture to a boil, then reduce the heat to low and simmer for 25-30 minutes, or until the lentils are tender.
4. Taste the soup and adjust seasoning if necessary. Ladle the soup into bowls and garnish with fresh parsley if desired. Serve hot with a slice of whole-grain bread if preferred.

---

Nutritional value (per serving):

Calories – 341 kcal
Protein – 15g
Carbohydrates – 50g
Sugars – 11g
Fibre – 17g
Fat – 9g
Saturated Fat – 1g

**Minimising Sugars:** Use fresh, whole ingredients and avoid pre-packaged or processed options. Ensure the chopped tomatoes are canned without added sugars.

**Enhancing Flavour:** Add a pinch of chilli flakes for a bit of heat. Incorporate fresh herbs like basil or coriander for additional flavour without extra sodium.

**Gluten-Free:** This recipe is naturally gluten-free.

**Vegan:** This recipe is already vegan, but you can add more vegetables like spinach or kale for added nutrition.

# Spinach and Mushroom Stuffed Bell Peppers

## Ingredients

- 2 large bell peppers (approximately 300g total)
- 1 tablespoon (15ml) extra virgin olive oil
- 1 medium onion (approximately 100g), finely chopped
- 2 cloves garlic, minced
- 200g fresh mushrooms, finely chopped
- 150g fresh spinach, roughly chopped
- 1 teaspoon dried oregano
- 1 teaspoon dried thyme
- 1/2 teaspoon ground black pepper
- 1/4 teaspoon salt (optional)
- 50g low-fat feta cheese, crumbled (optional)
- 1 tablespoon fresh parsley, chopped (for garnish)

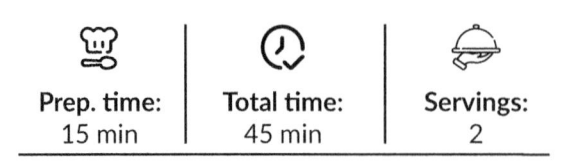

**Prep. time:** 15 min | **Total time:** 45 min | **Servings:** 2

## Directions

1. Preheat the oven to 180°C (350°F). Cut the bell peppers in half lengthwise and remove the seeds and membranes. Place the pepper halves on a baking tray, cut side up, and set aside.
2. In a large pan, heat the olive oil over medium heat. Add the chopped onion and minced garlic, and sauté for 3-4 minutes until the onion is translucent. Add the chopped mushrooms to the pan and cook for another 5 minutes until the mushrooms release their moisture and start to brown. Add the chopped spinach to the pan and cook until wilted, about 2-3 minutes. Season the mixture with dried oregano, dried thyme, ground black pepper, and salt (if using). Stir well to combine all ingredients.
3. Spoon the spinach and mushroom mixture evenly into the prepared bell pepper halves. If using feta cheese, sprinkle the crumbled cheese over the stuffed peppers.
4. Place the baking tray in the preheated oven and bake for 25-30 minutes, until the peppers are tender, and the filling is heated through.
5. Remove the stuffed peppers from the oven and let them cool slightly before serving. Garnish with freshly chopped parsley.

Nutritional value (per serving):

Calories – 195 kcal
Protein – 7g
Carbohydrates – 17g
Sugars – 9g
Fibre – 5g
Fat – 11g
Saturated Fat – 3g

**Minimising Sugars:** Use fresh, whole vegetables and avoid any pre-packaged options that may contain added sugars.

Opt for low-sodium options or eliminate added salt if monitoring sodium intake.

**Enhancing Flavour:** Add a pinch of chilli flakes for a bit of heat. Incorporate fresh herbs like basil or coriander for additional flavour without extra sodium.

**Gluten-Free:** This recipe is naturally gluten-free.

**Vegan:** Omit the feta cheese or substitute with a vegan cheese alternative.

# Chickpea and Tuna Salad with Lemon Vinaigrette

## Ingredients

**For the Salad:**
- 200g canned chickpeas, drained and rinsed
- 150g canned tuna in water, drained
- 1/2 cucumber (about 100g), diced
- 1 medium tomato (about 150g), diced
- 1/4 red onion (about 25g), finely chopped
- 30g mixed salad greens (e.g., lettuce, spinach)
- 10g fresh parsley, chopped
- 10g fresh coriander (cilantro), chopped (optional)

**For the Lemon Vinaigrette:**
- 2 tablespoons (30ml) extra virgin olive oil
- 1 tablespoon (15ml) fresh lemon juice
- 1/2 teaspoon Dijon mustard
- Salt and pepper, to taste

**Prep. time:** 15 min | **Total time:** 15 min | **Servings:** 2

## Directions

1. In a large mixing bowl, combine the drained chickpeas, canned tuna, diced cucumber, diced tomato, chopped red onion, mixed salad greens, fresh parsley, and optional fresh coriander.
2. In a small bowl, whisk together the extra virgin olive oil, fresh lemon juice, Dijon mustard, salt, and pepper until well combined.
3. Pour the lemon vinaigrette over the salad ingredients in the mixing bowl. Gently toss the salad until all ingredients are well coated with the vinaigrette
4. Divide the chickpea and tuna salad evenly between two serving plates or bowls.

---

Nutritional value (per serving):

Calories – 318 kcal
Protein – 21g
Carbohydrates – 18g
Sugars – 4g
Fibre – 6g
Fat – 18g
Saturated Fat – 3g

---

**Minimising Sugars:** Ensure the canned tuna is in water, not in oil, to avoid unnecessary fats and sugars.

**Enhancing Flavour:** Use fresh herbs like parsley and coriander to add flavour without extra sodium. Adjust the amount of lemon juice and mustard to balance the acidity and tanginess of the vinaigrette.

**Gluten-Free:** This recipe is naturally gluten-free.

**Vegan:** Substitute the tuna with cooked chickpeas or white beans for a plant-based version.

# Baked Sweet Potato with Greek Yoghurt and Chives

### Ingredients

- 2 medium sweet potatoes (about 300g each)
- 150g Greek yogurt (low-fat)
- 10g fresh chives, finely chopped
- Salt and pepper, to taste
- Olive oil spray (or 1 teaspoon olive oil)
- Optional: Fresh herbs such as parsley or thyme for garnish

**Prep. time:** 10 min | **Total time:** 55 min | **Servings:** 2

### Directions

1. Preheat your oven to 200°C (400°F).
2. Scrub the sweet potatoes thoroughly under cold water to remove any dirt. Pat them dry with a paper towel. Prick each sweet potato several times with a fork to allow steam to escape while baking.
3. Place the sweet potatoes on a baking tray lined with parchment paper. Spray each sweet potato lightly with olive oil or rub with a small amount of olive oil. Bake in the preheated oven for about 45 minutes, or until the sweet potatoes are tender and can be easily pierced with a fork.
4. While the sweet potatoes are baking, prepare the topping. In a small bowl, combine the Greek yogurt and chopped chives. Season with salt and pepper to taste. Mix well.
5. Once the sweet potatoes are baked, remove them from the oven and let them cool slightly for handling. Make a split lengthwise on the top of each sweet potato. Fluff the insides with a fork to create space for the topping. Spoon the Greek yogurt and chive mixture evenly onto each sweet potato.
6. Garnish with additional chopped chives and fresh herbs if desired. Serve the baked sweet potatoes immediately while warm.

---

**Nutritional value (per serving):**

Calories – 248 kcal
Protein – 7g
Carbohydrates – 46g
Sugars – 9g
Fibre – 7g
Fat – 4g
Saturated Fat – 1.5g

**Minimising Sugars:** Avoid adding any additional sugars or syrups to the sweet potatoes. Choose plain Greek yogurt without added sugars.

**Enhancing Flavour:** Fresh herbs like chives provide flavour without extra sodium. Consider adding a squeeze of fresh lemon juice for additional brightness.

**Gluten-Free:** This recipe is naturally gluten-free.

**Vegan:** Substitute Greek yogurt with a dairy-free alternative like coconut yogurt or hummus.

# Zucchini Noodles with Pesto and Cherry Tomatoes

## Ingredients

- 2 medium zucchinis (about 300g total)
- 150g cherry tomatoes, halved
- 30g pesto sauce (homemade or store-bought)
- 20g Parmesan cheese, grated (optional)
- 10g pine nuts, toasted (optional)
- Fresh basil leaves, thinly sliced, for garnish
- Salt and pepper, to taste
- Olive oil spray (or 1 teaspoon olive oil)

**Prep. time:** 15 min | **Total time:** 25 min | **Servings:** 2

## Directions

1. Using a spiralizer or vegetable peeler, create zucchini noodles (zoodles). If using a vegetable peeler, create long, thin strips resembling noodles. Place the zucchini noodles in a colander, sprinkle with a little salt, and let them sit for about 10 minutes. This helps to draw out excess moisture. Rinse thoroughly and pat dry with paper towels.
2. Heat a large non-stick pan over medium heat. Lightly spray with olive oil or use 1 teaspoon of olive oil. Add the zucchini noodles to the pan and sauté for 3-4 minutes, tossing gently, until they are just tender but still crisp. Be careful not to overcook. Remove from heat and set aside.
3. While the zucchini noodles are cooking, heat a small non-stick pan over medium heat. Add the halved cherry tomatoes to the pan and cook for 2-3 minutes, stirring occasionally, until they are slightly softened and heated through. Remove from heat and set aside.
4. In a large bowl, combine the cooked zucchini noodles and cherry tomatoes. Add the pesto sauce and toss gently until everything is evenly coated.
5. Divide the zucchini noodle mixture between two serving plates. If desired, sprinkle with grated Parmesan cheese and toasted pine nuts. Garnish with fresh basil leaves and season with salt and pepper to taste.

Nutritional value (per serving):

Calories – 195 kcal (without optional ingredients) or 243 kcal
Protein – 5g or 8g
Carbohydrates – 10g
Sugars – 5g
Fibre – 3g
Fat – 15g or 19g
Saturated Fat – 3g or 4g

**Minimising Sugars:** Use a homemade or store-bought pesto sauce with minimal added sugars.

**Enhancing Flavour:** Fresh basil and toasted pine nuts add flavour without extra sodium or sugar. Use a small amount of salt and pepper to enhance taste.

**Gluten-Free:** This recipe is naturally gluten-free.

**Vegan:** Substitute Greek yogurt with a dairy-free alternative like coconut yogurt or hummus.

# Chicken and Vegetable Stir-Fry

### Ingredients

- 250g chicken breast, thinly sliced
- 200g mixed vegetables (such as bell peppers, broccoli, carrots), sliced or cut into bite-sized pieces
- 1 medium onion, sliced
- 2 cloves garlic, minced
- 1 tbsp olive oil
- Salt and pepper to taste
- 1 tbsp low-sodium soy sauce
- 1 tbsp oyster sauce (optional)
- 1 tsp cornstarch mixed with 2 tbsp water (optional, for thickening)
- Fresh herbs (e.g., coriander, parsley) for garnish

**Prep. time:** 15 min | **Total time:** 30 min | **Servings:** 2

### Directions

1. Slice the chicken breast into thin strips. Prepare the vegetables by slicing or cutting them into bite-sized pieces.
2. Heat olive oil in a large pan or wok over medium-high heat.
3. Add the sliced chicken breast to the hot pan. Stir-fry for 4-5 minutes until the chicken is cooked through and lightly browned. Remove from the pan and set aside.
4. In the same pan, add the minced garlic and sliced onion. Stir-fry for 1-2 minutes until fragrant and the onion begins to soften. Add the mixed vegetables to the pan. Stir-fry for another 3-4 minutes until the vegetables are tender-crisp.
5. Return the cooked chicken to the pan with the vegetables. Stir well to combine.
6. Season with salt and pepper to taste. Add low- sodium soy sauce and oyster sauce (if using). Stir to coat evenly.
7. If a thicker sauce is desired, stir in the cornstarch mixture. Cook for another minute until the sauce thickens slightly.
8. Divide the chicken and vegetable stir-fry between two plates. Garnish with fresh herbs like coriander or parsley.

---

Nutritional value (per serving): without optional ingredients:

Calories – 278 kcal (with optional ingredients)
Protein – 33g
Carbohydrates – 14g
Sugars – 6g
Fibre – 3g
Fat – 10g
Saturated Fat – 1.5g

**Minimising Sugars:** Ensure soy sauce and oyster sauce are without added sugar.

**Enhancing Flavour:** Enhance flavour without extra sodium by using fresh herbs like basil or thyme, or spices like ginger or chilli flakes.

**Gluten-Free:** Ensure soy sauce and oyster sauce are gluten- free or use tamari as a substitute.

**Vegan:** Substitute chicken with tofu or tempeh and use vegan- friendly sauces.

# Tomato and Basil Soup with a Side of Whole Grain Bread

## Ingredients

- 500g ripe tomatoes, chopped
- 1 medium onion, finely chopped
- 2 cloves garlic, minced
- 1 tbsp olive oil
- 500ml low-sodium vegetable stock
- 10g fresh basil leaves, chopped
- Salt and pepper to taste
- 1 tsp balsamic vinegar (optional)
- 1 tbsp tomato paste (no added sugar)
- 1 tsp dried oregano
- 2 slices whole grain bread (approximately 60g each)

**Prep. time:** 10 min | **Total time:** 35 min | **Servings:** 2

## Directions

1. Chop the tomatoes, onion, and garlic. Wash and chop the fresh basil leaves.
2. In a large pot, heat the olive oil over medium heat. Add the chopped onion and garlic, and sauté for 3-4 minutes until the onion is translucent.
3. Add the chopped tomatoes to the pot and cook for about 5 minutes, stirring occasionally. Stir in the tomato paste and cook for another 2 minutes. Pour in the low-sodium vegetable stock and add the dried oregano. Bring the mixture to a boil, then reduce the heat and let it simmer for 15 minutes.
4. Using a hand blender or a countertop blender, blend the soup until smooth. If using a countertop blender, blend in batches if necessary. Return the blended soup to the pot and reheat gently.
5. Stir in the chopped basil leaves and season with salt and pepper to taste. Add the balsamic vinegar if desired for a touch of sweetness. Ladle the soup into bowls.
6. Toast the whole grain bread slices until golden brown.
7. Serve each bowl of soup with a slice of toasted whole grain bread on the side.

---

Nutritional value (per serving):

Calories – 250 kcal (without optional ingredients)
Protein – 6g
Carbohydrates – 34g
Sugars – 11g
Fibre – 6g
Fat – 10g
Saturated Fat – 1.5g

**Minimising Sugars:** Use fresh, ripe tomatoes and avoid canned tomatoes with added sugars. Opt for whole grain bread with no added sugars.

**Enhancing Flavour:** Use fresh herbs like basil and oregano for added flavour without extra sodium or sugar.

**Gluten-Free:** Use gluten-free bread instead of whole grain bread.

**Vegan:** This recipe is already vegan, but ensure the bread is also vegan-friendly if desired.

# 4 - NUTRITIOUS DINNER

## Planning Balanced Meals: Strategies for Dinner

When planning dinner for those with diabetes, it is crucial to focus on creating balanced meals that help maintain stable blood sugar levels. Dinner, being the last meal of the day, plays a significant role in ensuring overnight glycaemic control and setting the stage for the next day's metabolic processes.

### 1. Prioritising Low Glycaemic Index (GI) Foods

The glycaemic index (GI) measures how quickly foods raise blood sugar levels. For diabetics, choosing low-GI foods can help prevent spikes in blood sugar. For dinner, consider incorporating:

- LWhole grains: Quinoa, barley, and brown rice are excellent options.
- Non-starchy vegetables: Leafy greens, broccoli, cauliflower, and peppers are nutrient-dense and have a low GI.
- Legumes: Beans, lentils, and chickpeas are high in protein and fibre, contributing to a slower release of glucose.

### 2. Balancing Macronutrients

A well-balanced dinner should include a mix of carbohydrates, proteins, and fats. Each macronutrient plays a vital role in maintaining overall health and managing diabetes.

- Carbohydrates: Should come primarily from low-GI sources like vegetables, whole grains, and legumes. Keep portions moderate to avoid excessive blood sugar increases.
- Proteins: Lean proteins such as chicken, turkey, fish, tofu, and legumes help with satiety and blood sugar stability.
- Fats: Healthy fats from sources like olive oil, avocados, nuts, and seeds can enhance the meal's flavour and
- provide essential fatty acids without causing blood sugar spikes.

### 3. Portion Control

Portion control is key in managing diabetes. Even healthy foods can contribute to elevated blood sugar levels if consumed in enormous quantities. Use the plate method as a visual guide:

- Half the plate: Non-starchy vegetables
- A quarter of the plate: Lean protein
- A quarter of the plate: Whole grains or starchy vegetables

## 4. Incorporating Fibre

Fibre slows the absorption of sugar, helping to keep blood sugar levels stable. Aim to include plenty of high-fibre foods such as vegetables, legumes, whole grains, and fruits with low GI like berries and apples.

## 5. Choosing Healthy Cooking Methods

Opt for cooking methods that do not add unnecessary fats or sugars to your meal. Ideal methods include:

- Grilling: Ideal for lean proteins and vegetables.
- Steaming: Retains nutrients in vegetables without adding fat.
- Baking or roasting: Enhances flavour in vegetables and proteins without excessive oil.

## 6. Reducing Sodium and Enhancing Flavour

While sodium does not directly impact blood sugar, high sodium intake is linked to hypertension, which can complicate diabetes management. Instead of salt, use herbs, spices, and citrus to flavour your meals. Fresh herbs like basil, thyme, and

coriander, and spices such as cumin, paprika, and turmeric can add depth without sodium.

## 7. Planning Ahead

Meal planning can prevent impulsive, less healthy choices. Prepare a weekly menu, shop with a list, and consider batch cooking to save time. Having a plan ensures that you always have diabetes-friendly options on hand.

## 8. Mindful Eating

Pay attention to your body's hunger and fullness cues. Eating slowly and savouring your meal can prevent overeating and improve digestion. Avoid distractions such as TV or smartphones during meals to focus on the experience of eating.

Creating balanced meals for dinner involves thoughtful planning and an understanding of how different foods affect blood sugar levels. By prioritising low-GI foods, balancing macronutrients, controlling portions, and using healthy cooking methods, you can enjoy delicious and nutritious dinners that support optimal glycaemic control. Embracing these strategies will not only benefit those managing diabetes but can also promote overall health and well-being for everyone at the dinner table.

# Baked Salmon with Asparagus and Quinoa

## Ingredients

- 2 salmon fillets (approximately 150g each)
- 200g asparagus, trimmed
- 1 tablespoon olive oil (15ml)
- 1 lemon, sliced
- 1 teaspoon dried dill (5g)
- 1 teaspoon dried thyme (5g)
- Salt and pepper to taste
- 120g quinoa
- 240ml water
- 1 tablespoon olive oil (15ml)
- 1 garlic clove, minced
- 50g chopped red onion
- 50g chopped red bell pepper
- 1 tablespoon chopped fresh parsley (5g)

**Prep. time:** 15 min | **Total time:** 40 min | **Servings:** 2

## Directions

1. Preheat your oven to 200°C (180°C fan-assisted) or Gas Mark 6. Line a baking tray with parchment paper. Place the salmon fillets on the baking tray. Drizzle 1 tablespoon of olive oil over the salmon and sprinkle with dried dill, dried thyme, salt, and pepper. Place lemon slices on top of the salmon fillets. Arrange the asparagus spears around the salmon on the baking tray. Drizzle a little olive oil over the asparagus and season with salt and pepper. Bake in the preheated oven for 20-25 minutes, or until the salmon is cooked through and flakes easily with a fork, and the asparagus is tender.
2. Rinse the quinoa under cold water using a fine-mesh sieve to remove its natural bitterness. In a medium saucepan, bring 240ml of water to a boil. Add the quinoa, reduce the heat to low, cover, and simmer for 15 minutes, or until the water is absorbed and the quinoa is tender. Fluff the quinoa with a fork and set aside.
3. In a large frying pan, heat 1 tablespoon of olive oil over medium heat. Add the minced garlic, chopped red onion, and chopped red bell pepper. Sauté for 5-7 minutes, until the vegetables are tender. Add the cooked quinoa to the frying pan with the sautéed vegetables. Stir well to combine and heat through. Remove from heat and stir in the chopped fresh parsley.
4. Serve each salmon fillet alongside a portion of asparagus and a generous scoop of quinoa. Garnish with additional lemon wedges and a sprinkle of fresh herbs if desired.

---

Nutritional value (per serving):

Calories – 631 kcal
Protein – 42g
Carbohydrates – 37g
Sugars – 4g
Fibre – 6g
Fat – 35g
Saturated Fat – 6g

**Minimising Sugars:** Choose fresh, whole ingredients. Skip sugary marinades or sauces.

**Enhancing Flavour:** dried dill and thyme add flavour without adding sugar. Fresh parsley adds a burst of freshness and enhance the dish without extra sugar.

**Gluten-Free:** This recipe is naturally gluten-free.

**Vegan:** Substitute the salmon with large portobello mushrooms or a marinated tofu steak. Adjust the baking time, as necessary.

# Grilled Chicken with Steamed Broccoli and Brown Rice

## Ingredients

- 2 chicken breasts (approximately 150g each)
- 1 tablespoon olive oil (15ml)
- 1 teaspoon dried oregano (5g)
- 1 teaspoon dried thyme (5g)
- 1 teaspoon garlic powder (5g)
- Salt and pepper to taste
- 300g broccoli florets
- 1 tablespoon olive oil (15ml)
- 1 lemon, juiced
- Salt and pepper to taste
- 120g brown rice
- 240ml water

**Prep. time:** 15 min | **Total time:** 45 min | **Servings:** 2

## Directions

1. Preheat your grill to medium-high heat. In a small bowl, mix the olive oil, dried oregano, dried thyme, garlic powder, salt, and pepper. Brush the chicken breasts with this mixture.
2. Place the chicken breasts on the grill and cook for 6-8 minutes per side, or until the internal temperature reaches 75°C and the chicken is no longer pink in the centre. Remove the chicken from the grill and let it rest for 5 minutes before slicing.
3. Wash and cut the broccoli into florets. Place the broccoli florets in a steamer basket over boiling water. Cover and steam for 5-7 minutes, until tender but still bright green. Drizzle the steamed broccoli with olive oil and lemon juice, then season with salt and pepper.
4. Rinse the brown rice under cold water using a fine-mesh sieve. In a medium saucepan, bring 240ml of water to a boil. Add the brown rice, reduce the heat to low, cover, and simmer for 25-30 minutes, or until the water is absorbed and the rice is tender. Fluff the rice with a fork before serving.
5. Serve each plate with one grilled chicken breast, half of the steamed broccoli, and half of the cooked brown rice. Garnish with fresh herbs such as parsley or chives if desired.

Nutritional value (per serving):

Calories – 547 kcal
Protein – 42g
Carbohydrates – 43g
Sugars – 3g
Fibre – 5g
Fat – 23g
Saturated Fat – 3g

**Minimising Sugars:** Avoid sugary marinades or sauces.

**Enhancing Flavour:** Replace dried oregano and thyme with fresh herbs for a more vibrant taste.

**Gluten-Free:** This recipe is naturally gluten-free.

**Vegan:** Substitute the chicken with marinated tofu or tempeh and adjust the grilling time, as necessary.

# Stir-Fried Tofu with Mixed Vegetables

## Ingredients

**Stir-Fried Tofu:**
- 200g firm tofu, drained and cubed
- 1 tablespoon olive oil (15ml)
- 1 teaspoon low-sodium soy sauce (5ml)
- 1 teaspoon fresh ginger, grated (5g)
- 1 clove garlic, minced

**Mixed Vegetables:**
- 1 red bell pepper, sliced (120g)
- 1 yellow bell pepper, sliced (120g)
- 100g broccoli florets
- 100g snap peas
- 1 medium carrot, julienned (60g)
- 1 tablespoon olive oil (15ml)
- 1 tablespoon low-sodium soy sauce (15ml)
- 1 teaspoon sesame oil (5ml)
- 1 tablespoon rice vinegar (15ml)
- 1 teaspoon fresh ginger, grated (5g)
- 1 clove garlic, minced

**Prep. time:** 15 min | **Total time:** 35 min | **Servings:** 2

## Directions

1. Drain the tofu and pat dry with kitchen paper. Cut into cubes. In a bowl, mix 1 tablespoon of olive oil, 1 teaspoon of low-sodium soy sauce, 1 teaspoon of grated ginger, and 1 minced garlic clove. Add the tofu cubes and gently toss to coat. Let it marinate for 10 minutes. Heat a non-stick pan over medium heat. Add the marinated tofu and cook for 5-7 minutes, turning occasionally until all sides are golden brown. Remove from the pan and set aside.
2. Wash and slice the bell peppers, broccoli, snap peas, and carrot. In the same pan used for the tofu, add 1 tablespoon of olive oil and heat over medium-high heat. Add the ginger and garlic, and sauté for 1 minute until fragrant. Add the sliced bell peppers, broccoli, snap peas, and carrot to the pan. Stir-fry for 5-7 minutes until the vegetables are tender-crisp. Add 1 tablespoon of low-sodium soy sauce, 1 teaspoon of sesame oil, and 1 tablespoon of rice vinegar. Toss to combine and cook for an additional 2-3 minutes.
3. Return the cooked tofu to the pan with the vegetables. Toss everything together and cook for another 2 minutes to heat through.
4. Serve the stir-fried tofu and mixed vegetables on a plate. Garnish with fresh coriander or sesame seeds if desired. If desired, pair with a small portion of brown rice or quinoa for a complete meal, keeping in mind portion control.

**Nutritional value (per serving):**

Calories – 340 kcal
Protein – 11g
Carbohydrates – 20g
Sugars – 8g
Fibre – 5g
Fat – 24g
Saturated Fat – 3g

**Minimising Sugars:** Most ingredients are already low in sugar; stick to these types of vegetables. Ensure the soy sauce is low-sodium and avoid any sweetened varieties.

**Enhancing Flavour:** Add extra fresh ginger and garlic for a more robust flavour. Add a pinch of red chilli flakes or Sichuan peppercorns for heat.

**Gluten-Free:** Ensure the soy sauce is gluten-free.

**Vegan:** This recipe is naturally vegan.

# Turkey Meatballs with Zucchini Noodles

## Ingredients

**Turkey Meatballs:**
- 250g lean turkey mince
- 1 small onion, finely chopped (50g)
- 1 clove garlic, minced
- 1 medium egg, beaten
- 30g wholemeal breadcrumbs
- 1 tablespoon fresh parsley, chopped
- 1 teaspoon dried oregano
- 1/2 teaspoon black pepper
- 1/2 teaspoon paprika

**Zucchini Noodles:**
- 2 medium courgettes (zucchini), spiralised (400g)
- 1 tablespoon olive oil (15ml)
- 1 clove garlic, minced
- 100g cherry tomatoes, halved
- 1 tablespoon fresh basil, chopped

**Sauce:**
- 200g canned chopped tomatoes (no added salt or sugar)
- 1 tablespoon tomato puree
- 1 teaspoon dried oregano
- 1/2 teaspoon black pepper
- 1/2 teaspoon paprika

**Prep. time:** 20 min | **Total time:** 45 min | **Servings:** 2

## Directions

1. Preheat your oven to 200°C (180°C fan). In a large bowl, combine the turkey mince, chopped onion, minced garlic, beaten egg, wholemeal breadcrumbs, parsley, oregano, black pepper, and paprika. Mix well until all ingredients are thoroughly combined. Shape the mixture into small meatballs, about the size of a walnut, and place them on a baking tray lined with parchment paper. Bake in the preheated oven for 20 minutes, or until the meatballs are cooked through and golden brown.
2. While the meatballs are baking, heat a saucepan over medium heat. Add the canned chopped tomatoes, tomato puree, oregano, black pepper, and paprika. Stir to combine. Let the sauce simmer for about 10 minutes, stirring occasionally, until it thickens slightly.
3. Spiralise the courgettes to create zucchini noodles. If you do not have a spiraliser, you can use a vegetable peeler to create thin strips. Heat the olive oil in a large pan over medium heat. Add the minced garlic and cook for 1 minute until fragrant. Add the zucchini noodles and cherry tomatoes to the pan. Sauté for 3-4 minutes until the noodles are tender but still slightly firm. Stir in the chopped basil and remove from heat.
4. Add the baked turkey meatballs to the saucepan with the tomato sauce. Stir gently to coat the meatballs in the sauce. Divide the zucchini noodles between two plates. Top with the turkey meatballs and sauce.

**Nutritional value (per serving):**

Calories – 342 kcal
Protein – 30g
Carbohydrates – 24g
Sugars – 12g
Fibre – 6g
Fat – 14
Saturated Fat – 3g

**Minimising Sugars:** Ensure that canned tomatoes and tomato puree are unsweetened.

**Enhancing Flavour:** Use a teaspoon of nutritional yeast in the meatball mixture for a cheesy, umami flavour. A splash of balsamic vinegar in the sauce can add depth and a slight sweetness without added sugar.

**Gluten-Free:** Ensure the soy sauce is gluten-free.

**Vegan:** This recipe is naturally vegan.

# Baked Cod with Roasted Brussels Sprouts

## Ingredients

**Baked Cod:**
- 2 cod fillets (about 150g each)
- 1 tablespoon olive oil (15ml)
- 1 lemon (juice and zest)
- 1 teaspoon fresh thyme, chopped
- 1 clove garlic, minced
- 1/2 teaspoon black pepper
- 1/2 teaspoon paprika

**Roasted Brussels Sprouts:**
- 300g Brussels sprouts, halved
- 1 tablespoon olive oil (15ml)
- 1 teaspoon balsamic vinegar
- 1 teaspoon dried rosemary
- 1/2 teaspoon black pepper

**Prep. time:** 15 min | **Total time:** 45 min | **Servings:** 2

## Directions

1. Preheat your oven to 200°C (180°C fan). In a
2. small bowl, combine the olive oil, lemon juice and zest, chopped thyme, minced garlic, black pepper, and paprika. Mix well.
3. Place the cod fillets on a baking tray lined with parchment paper. Brush the marinade evenly over the fillets. Let them marinate for 10 minutes. Bake the cod in the preheated oven for 15-20 minutes, or until the fish flakes easily with a fork.
4. In a bowl, toss the halved Brussels sprouts with olive oil, balsamic vinegar, dried rosemary, and black pepper. Spread the Brussels sprouts on a baking tray lined with parchment paper.
5. Roast in the preheated oven for 25-30 minutes, or until they are golden brown and crispy, turning them halfway through cooking.

**Nutritional value (per serving):**

Calories – 371 kcal
Protein – 36g
Carbohydrates – 14g
Sugars – 2g
Fibre – 5g
Fat – 19g
Saturated Fat – 3g

**Minimising Sugars:** Use a smaller amount or choose a balsamic vinegar with no added sugars. Allow the natural caramelisation of Brussels sprouts to bring out their inherent sweetness instead of adding sugary ingredients.

**Enhancing Flavour:** Add lemon zest to both the cod and Brussels sprouts for a fresh, bright flavour. Incorporate fresh parsley or dill for additional herbal notes.

**Gluten-Free:** This recipe is naturally gluten-free.

**Vegan:** Substitute the cod with marinated tofu or a plant-based fish alternative and follow the same baking instructions.

# Vegetable Curry with Cauliflower Rice

## Ingredients

**Vegetable Curry:**
- 1 tablespoon olive oil (15ml)
- 1 medium onion, finely chopped (100g)
- 2 cloves garlic, minced
- 1 tablespoon fresh ginger, grated
- 1 red bell pepper, chopped (150g)
- 1 courgette, chopped (200g)
- 100g carrots, chopped
- 200g tinned chickpeas, drained and rinsed
- 200ml tinned tomatoes, chopped
- 200ml coconut milk (light)
- 1 tablespoon curry powder
- 1 teaspoon ground cumin
- 1 teaspoon ground coriander
- 1/2 teaspoon turmeric
- 1/2 teaspoon black pepper
- 1/2 teaspoon ground cinnamon
- 100g fresh spinach

**Cauliflower Rice:**
- 1 medium cauliflower (500g)
- 1 tablespoon olive oil (15ml)
- 1/2 teaspoon black pepper
- 1/2 teaspoon ground turmeric

**Prep. time:** 20 min | **Total time:** 50 min | **Servings:** 2

## Directions

1. In a large pan, heat the olive oil over medium heat. Add the chopped onion, garlic, and grated ginger. Sauté for 3-4 minutes until the onion is translucent.
2. Add the chopped red bell pepper, courgette, and carrots. Cook for another 5 minutes, stirring occasionally. Stir in the curry powder, ground cumin, ground coriander, turmeric, black pepper, and ground cinnamon. Cook for 1 minute to release the flavours.
3. Add the tinned tomatoes, coconut milk, and chickpeas. Stir well to combine. Bring the mixture to a boil, then reduce the heat to low and let it simmer for 20 minutes, or until the vegetables are tender. Stir in the fresh spinach and cook for an additional 2-3 minutes until wilted.
4. Remove the leaves and core from the cauliflower. Cut into florets and pulse in a food processor until it resembles rice.
5. In a large pan, heat the olive oil over medium heat. Add the cauliflower rice, black pepper, and ground turmeric. Sauté for 5-7 minutes until tender.

---

Nutritional value (per serving):

Calories – 458 kcal
Protein – 12g
Carbohydrates – 44g
Sugars – 17g
Fibre – 14g
Fat – 26g
Saturated Fat – 13.5g

**Minimising Sugars:** Opt for unsweetened coconut milk. Select tinned tomatoes without added sugar.

**Enhancing Flavour:** Fresh coriander (coriander), mint, or basil can elevate the dish's taste significantly. Add them at the end of cooking for a burst of freshness.

**Gluten-Free:** This recipe is naturally gluten-free.

**Vegan:** This recipe is vegan-friendly.

# Lean Beef Stir-Fry with Bell Peppers and Snow Peas

## Ingredients

- 200g lean beef steak, thinly sliced
- 1 tablespoon olive oil (15ml)
- 1 medium red bell pepper, sliced (150g)
- 1 medium yellow bell pepper, sliced (150g)
- 100g snow peas, trimmed
- 1 medium onion, thinly sliced (100g)
- 2 cloves garlic, minced
- 1 tablespoon fresh ginger, grated
- 2 tablespoons low-sodium soy sauce (30ml)
- 1 tablespoon rice vinegar (15ml)
- 1 tablespoon sesame oil (15ml)
- 1 teaspoon cornflour (5g) mixed with 2 tablespoons water (30ml)
- 1 teaspoon black pepper
- 1 teaspoon ground coriander
- 1 tablespoon sesame seeds (optional, for garnish)
- Fresh coriander (optional, for garnish)

**Prep. time:** 15 min | **Total time:** 30 min | **Servings:** 2

## Directions

1. Slice the beef steak into thin strips, and cut the bell peppers, onion, and snow peas. Mince the garlic and grate the ginger. In a bowl, combine the beef strips with 1 tablespoon of low-sodium soy sauce, black pepper, and ground coriander. Let it marinate for 10 minutes.
2. In a large wok or frying pan, heat the olive oil over medium-high heat. Add the marinated beef strips to the hot wok and stir-fry for 2-3 minutes until browned. Remove the beef from the wok and set aside.
3. In the same wok, add the sliced onion, garlic, and ginger. Stir-fry for 2 minutes until fragrant. Add the sliced bell peppers and snow peas to the wok. Stir-fry for 3-4 minutes until the vegetables are tender-crisp. Return the beef to the wok with the vegetables. Add the remaining 1 tablespoon of soy sauce, rice vinegar, and sesame oil. Stir well to combine.
4. Add the cornflour mixture to the wok, stirring constantly until the sauce thickens and coats the beef and vegetables evenly.
5. Transfer the stir-fry to serving plates. Garnish with sesame seeds and fresh coriander if desired.

---

Nutritional value (per serving):

Calories – 507 kcal
Protein – 33g
Carbohydrates – 24g
Sugars – 10g
Fibre – 5g
Fat – 31g
Saturated Fat – 9g

---

**Minimising Sugars:** Use fresh ingredients. Avoid sweet sauces and ingredients.

**Enhancing Flavour:** Enhance the flavour by increasing the amount of garlic and ginger. These aromatics add depth without adding sugar. Incorporate ingredients rich in umami like mushrooms or add a small amount of fish sauce. These ingredients add a savoury depth that complements the beef.

**Gluten-Free:** Use gluten-free soy sauce or tamari.

**Vegan:** Replace the beef with tofu or tempeh and adjust cooking times accordingly.

# Herb-Crusted Pork Tenderloin with Green Beans

## Ingredients

- 300g pork tenderloin
- 1 tablespoon olive oil (15ml)
- 2 teaspoons Dijon mustard (10ml)
- 1 tablespoon fresh parsley, chopped (5g)
- 1 tablespoon fresh thyme, chopped (5g)
- 1 tablespoon fresh rosemary, chopped (5g)
- 1 teaspoon garlic powder (5g)
- 1 teaspoon black pepper (5g)
- 1 teaspoon sea salt (5g)
- 200g green beans, trimmed
- 1 lemon, sliced
- 1 tablespoon lemon juice (15ml)
- 1 tablespoon water (15ml)

**Prep. time:** 15 min | **Total time:** 40 min | **Servings:** 2

## Directions

1. Preheat your oven to 200°C (180°C fan).
2. Pat the pork tenderloin dry with paper towels. Brush it evenly with Dijon mustard. In a small bowl, mix the chopped parsley, thyme, rosemary, garlic powder, black pepper, and sea salt. Press this herb mixture onto the mustard-coated pork, ensuring an even coating.
3. Transfer the skillet to the preheated oven. Bake for 15-20 minutes, or until the internal temperature of the pork reaches 70°C. Remove the pork from the oven and let it rest for 5 minutes before slicing.
4. While the pork is baking, steam the green beans. In a pot with a steamer insert, bring water to a boil. Add the green beans, cover, and steam for 4-5 minutes until tender-crisp. In a small bowl, mix the lemon juice and water. Drizzle over the steamed green beans.
5. Slice the herb-crusted pork tenderloin and serve with the steamed green beans. Garnish with lemon slices if desired.

---

Nutritional value (per serving):

Calories – 325 kcal
Protein – 28g
Carbohydrates – 15g
Sugars – 4g
Fibre – 5g
Fat – 17g
Saturated Fat – 4g

**Minimising Sugars:** Use fresh ingredients. Avoid sweet sauces and ingredients.

**Enhancing Flavour:** Add more fresh parsley, thyme, and rosemary to elevate the herbal flavour profile. Fresh herbs add vibrant flavours without adding sugar. Incorporate fresh garlic instead of garlic powder for a stronger, more nuanced flavour. Consider adding finely chopped onions or shallots as well.

**Gluten-Free:** This recipe is naturally gluten-free.

**Vegan:** Replace the pork tenderloin with a plant-based meat substitute or portobello mushrooms, adjusting cooking times as needed.

# Stuffed Portobello Mushrooms with Spinach and Cheese

## Ingredients

- 4 large Portobello mushrooms (approximately 300g)
- 1 tablespoon olive oil (15ml)
- 1 small onion, finely chopped (100g)
- 2 cloves garlic, minced
- 150g fresh spinach, washed and chopped
- 100g ricotta cheese
- 50g grated mozzarella cheese
- 30g grated Parmesan cheese
- 1 teaspoon dried oregano (5g)
- 1 teaspoon dried basil (5g)
- 1/2 teaspoon black pepper (2.5g)
- 1/4 teaspoon sea salt (1.5g)

**Prep. time:** 15 min | **Total time:** 35 min | **Servings:** 2

## Directions

1. Preheat your oven to 200°C (180°C fan).
2. Clean the Portobello mushrooms by wiping them with a damp cloth. Remove the stems and gently scrape out the gills with a spoon to create a cavity for the stuffing. Place the mushrooms on a baking tray lined with parchment paper.
3. In a large frying pan, heat the olive oil over medium heat. Add the chopped onion and garlic, and sauté until the onion becomes translucent, about 5 minutes. Add the chopped spinach to the pan and cook until it wilts, about 3 minutes. Remove from heat and let it cool slightly.
4. In a mixing bowl, combine the cooked spinach mixture, ricotta cheese, half of the grated mozzarella cheese, Parmesan cheese, dried oregano, dried basil, black pepper, and sea salt. Mix well to combine. Spoon the filling evenly into the prepared mushroom caps. Sprinkle the remaining grated mozzarella cheese on top of each stuffed mushroom.
5. Bake in the preheated oven for 15-20 minutes, or until the mushrooms are tender and the cheese is melted and golden. Remove from the oven and let cool slightly before serving. Enjoy these stuffed Portobello mushrooms as a main dish or a hearty side.

---

Nutritional value (per serving):

Calories – 366 kcal
Protein – 20g
Carbohydrates – 22g
Sugars – 8g
Fibre – 7g
Fat – 22g
Saturated Fat – 11g

**Minimising Sugars:** Use fresh ingredients. Avoid sweet sauces and ingredients.

**Enhancing Flavour:** Sprinkle some toasted pine nuts or sunflower seeds on top of the stuffed mushrooms for a crunchy texture and nutty flavour.

**Gluten-Free:** This recipe is naturally gluten-free.

**Vegan:** Replace the ricotta, mozzarella, and Parmesan cheese with vegan cheese alternatives and ensure the olive oil is vegan-friendly.

# Spaghetti Squash with Marinara and Turkey Meat Sauce

## Ingredients

- 1 medium spaghetti squash (approximately 900g)
- 1 tablespoon olive oil (15ml)
- 1 small onion, finely chopped (100g)
- 2 cloves garlic, minced
- 250g lean ground turkey
- 400g canned chopped tomatoes (no added sugar)
- 1 tablespoon tomato paste (15g)
- 1 teaspoon dried oregano (5g)
- 1 teaspoon dried basil (5g)
- 1/2 teaspoon dried thyme (2.5g)
- 1/2 teaspoon black pepper (2.5g)
- 1/4 teaspoon sea salt (1.5g)
- 30g grated Parmesan cheese (optional)
- Fresh basil leaves for garnish (optional)

**Prep. time:** 15 min | **Total time:** 60 min | **Servings:** 2

## Directions

1. Preheat your oven to 200°C (180°C fan).
2. Cut the spaghetti squash in half lengthwise and scoop out the seeds. Place the squash halves cut side down on a baking tray lined with parchment paper. Bake in the preheated oven for 30-35 minutes, or until the flesh is tender and easily scraped into strands with a fork.
3. While the squash is baking, heat the olive oil in a large frying pan over medium heat. Add the chopped onion and garlic, and sauté until the onion becomes translucent, about 5 minutes. Add the ground turkey to the pan with the onion and garlic. Cook, breaking up the meat with a spoon, until it is no longer pink, about 7-10 minutes.
4. Stir in the canned chopped tomatoes, tomato paste, dried oregano, dried basil, dried thyme, black pepper, and sea salt. Bring the mixture to a simmer and cook for 15 minutes, stirring occasionally, to allow the flavours to meld.
5. Once the squash is cooked, remove it from the oven and let it cool slightly. Using a fork, scrape the flesh of the squash to create spaghetti-like strands. Place the strands in a serving bowl.
6. Top the spaghetti squash with the turkey marinara sauce. If using, sprinkle with grated Parmesan cheese and garnish with fresh basil leaves. Serve immediately.

Nutritional value (per serving):

Calories – 396 kcal (without optional ingredients) or 460 (with optional ingredients) kcal
Protein – 25g or 31g
Carbohydrates – 38g or 39g
Sugars – 17g
Fibre – 9g
Fat – 16g or 20g
Saturated Fat – 3g or 6g

**Minimising Sugars:** Use fresh ingredients. Avoid sweet sauces and ingredients.

**Enhancing Flavour:** Sprinkle some toasted pine nuts or sunflower seeds on top of the stuffed mushrooms for a crunchy texture and nutty flavour.

**Gluten-Free:** This recipe is naturally gluten-free.

**Vegan:** Replace the ground turkey with crumbled tofu or a plant-based meat alternative and ensure the Parmesan cheese is vegan-friendly or omit it.

# 5 – SMART SNACKING

## Healthy Snack Options: Managing Cravings

Cravings can be particularly challenging for individuals managing diabetes. The key to managing these cravings effectively lies in smart snacking. Choosing snacks that are not only delicious but also align with glycaemic control principles is crucial for maintaining stable blood sugar levels. This subchapter will explore healthy snack options and strategies to manage cravings, ensuring you can enjoy your snacks without compromising your health.

### Understanding Cravings

Cravings are intense desires for specific foods, often high in sugar, fat, or salt. They can be triggered by numerous factors, including stress, hormonal changes, or simply the sight and smell of certain foods. For diabetics, giving in to unhealthy cravings can lead to significant blood sugar spikes, making it essential to find satisfying yet healthy alternatives.

### Strategies for Managing Cravings

1. Identify Triggers:

Understanding what triggers your cravings is the first step in managing them. Keep a food diary to note when and what you crave, along with any emotional or environmental triggers.

2. Stay Hydrated:

Sometimes, what we perceive as hunger or cravings can actually be thirst. Drinking a glass of water before reaching for a snack can help determine if you are truly hungry.

3. Regular Meals:

Eating balanced meals at regular intervals can prevent extreme hunger that often leads to cravings. Each meal should include a mix of protein, healthy fats, and low-GI carbohydrates.

4. Healthy Substitutes:

Find healthier alternatives for your favourite snacks. For instance, if you crave something sweet, opt for a small piece of dark chocolate or some fruit. If you crave something salty, try roasted nuts instead of crisps.

### Tips for Choosing Snacks

1. Focus on Nutrient-Dense Foods:

Choose snacks that offer vitamins, minerals, and other nutrients rather than empty calories.

2. Combine Macronutrients:

Combining protein, fat, and carbohydrates in your snacks can help you feel fuller longer and maintain stable blood sugar levels.

3. Watch Portions:

Even healthy snacks can contribute to weight gain and blood sugar spikes if eaten in massive quantities. Stick to recommended serving sizes.

4. Read Labels:

Check the nutritional information on packaged snacks to avoid hidden sugars and unhealthy fats.

## **Snack Planning for Diabetics**

1. Prepare in Advance:

Having healthy snacks prepared and ready can prevent you from reaching for less healthy options. Keep cut vegetables, portioned nuts, and other healthy snacks readily available.

2. Include Snacks in Your Meal Plan:

Incorporate snacks into your daily meal plan to account for their nutritional content and avoid overconsumption.

3. Mindful Eating:

Practice mindful eating by paying attention to your snack choices and eating slowly to enjoy and savour each bite.

# Hummus with Cucumber and Carrot Sticks

**Prep. time:** 15 min | **Total time:** 15 min | **Servings:** 2

## Ingredients

**For the Hummus:**
- 240g canned chickpeas (drained and rinsed)
- 2 tablespoons tahini (30g)
- 1 small garlic clove, minced
- 2 tablespoons fresh lemon juice (30ml)
- 1 tablespoon olive oil (15ml)
- 1/2 teaspoon ground cumin (2.5g)
- 1/4 teaspoon sea salt (1.5g)
- 2-3 tablespoons water (30-45ml), as needed for consistency

**For the Vegetable Sticks:**
- 1 medium cucumber (approx. 200g)
- 2 medium carrots (approx. 150g)

## Directions

1. Place the chickpeas, tahini, minced garlic, lemon juice, olive oil, ground cumin, and sea salt into a food processor.
2. Blend the ingredients until smooth, adding water gradually until the hummus reaches your desired consistency.
3. Taste and adjust the seasoning if needed, adding more lemon juice or salt to taste.
4. Wash the cucumber and carrots thoroughly.
5. Peel the carrots and cut them into sticks about 7-10cm long.
6. Cut the cucumber into similar-sized sticks.
7. Divide the hummus into two small bowls.
8. Arrange the cucumber and carrot sticks on a plate around the hummus.

**Nutritional value (per serving):**

Calories – 377 kcal
Protein – 13g
Carbohydrates – 43g
Sugars – 10g
Fibre – 11g
Fat – 17g
Saturated Fat – 2g

**Serving Suggestions:** Pair with a small portion of whole-grain crackers for added fibre. Serve with a side salad for a more filling snack.

**Enhancing Flavour:** Use fresh herbs like parsley or coriander to garnish the hummus. Add a pinch of paprika or a drizzle of extra virgin olive oil on top of the hummus for added flavour.

**Gluten-Free:** This recipe is naturally gluten-free.

**Vegan:** This recipe is naturally vegan.

# Apple Slices with Almond Butter

## Ingredients

- 2 medium apples (approximately 300g each)
- 4 tablespoons (60g) almond butter
- 1 teaspoon ground cinnamon (optional, for extra flavour)

**Prep. time:** 10 min | **Total time:** 10 min | **Servings:** 2

## Directions

1. Wash the apples thoroughly under running water. Core the apples and cut them into thin slices (about 1 cm thick). Each apple should yield 8-10 slices.
2. Measure 2 tablespoons (30g) of almond butter for each serving. If desired, you can gently warm the almond butter in a microwave-safe dish for about 10-15 seconds to make it easier to spread.
3. Arrange the apple slices on a serving plate. Spread 2 tablespoons (30g) of almond butter on a few of the apple slices or use it as a dip.
4. Sprinkle a pinch of ground cinnamon over the apple slices and almond butter for added flavour and a touch of spice.
5. Divide the apple slices between two plates, ensuring each serving has an equal portion of almond butter.

Nutritional value (per serving):

Calories – 366.5 kcal
Protein – 7.5g
Carbohydrates – 47g
Sugars – 31g
Fibre – 12g
Fat – 16.5g
Saturated Fat – 1.5g

**Tips for Glycaemic Control:** Choose apples that are lower in natural sugars, such as Granny Smith apples, which have a lower glycaemic index compared to sweeter varieties like Gala or Fuji. Ensure the almond butter is unsweetened and does not contain added sugars or hydrogenated oils.

**Serving Suggestions:** For a more balanced snack, consider pairing this with a small serving of Greek yoghurt (if not vegan) or a handful of unsalted nuts.

**Gluten-Free:** This recipe is naturally gluten-free.

**Vegan:** This recipe is naturally vegan.

# Greek Yoghurt with Walnuts and Fresh Berries

## Ingredients

- 200g plain Greek yoghurt (low-fat)
- 50g fresh blueberries
- 50g fresh raspberries
- 30g walnuts, roughly chopped
- 1 teaspoon vanilla extract (optional, for added flavour)
- 1 teaspoon ground cinnamon (optional, for added flavour)

**Prep. time:** 10 min | **Total time:** 10 min | **Servings:** 2

## Directions

1. Rinse the blueberries and raspberries under cold water and pat dry. Roughly chop the walnuts.
2. Divide the Greek yoghurt equally into two bowls (100g per bowl). If using, mix the vanilla extract into the yoghurt for added flavour.
3. Top each bowl of yoghurt with 25g of blueberries and 25g of raspberries. Sprinkle 15g of chopped walnuts over each bowl.
4. Sprinkle a pinch of ground cinnamon over the yoghurt and fruit for an extra layer of flavour.
5. Serve immediately to enjoy the freshness of the berries and the crunch of the walnuts.

---

**Nutritional value (per serving):**

- Calories – 196.3 kcal
- Protein – 12.8g
- Carbohydrates – 13.1g
- Sugars – 8.1g
- Fibre – 4.2g
- Fat – 10.3g
- Saturated Fat – 1g

**Tips for Glycaemic Control:** Choose plain Greek yoghurt without added sugars. Greek yoghurt is preferred due to its higher protein content, which helps with satiety and blood sugar control.

**Serving Suggestions:** Pair this snack with a small serving of lean protein, such as a boiled egg, for additional protein and to further stabilise blood sugar levels.

**Gluten-Free:** This recipe is naturally gluten-free.

**Vegan:** Substitute Greek yoghurt with a plant-based yoghurt, such as coconut or almond yoghurt, making sure it is unsweetened and low in added sugars.

# Roasted Chickpeas with Paprika

## Ingredients

- 1 can (400g) chickpeas, drained and rinsed (240g drained weight)
- 1 tablespoon olive oil (15ml)
- 1 teaspoon paprika (5g)
- 1/2 teaspoon ground cumin (2.5g)
- 1/4 teaspoon garlic powder (1.25g)
- 1/4 teaspoon onion powder (1.25g)
- 1/4 teaspoon sea salt (1.25g)
- 1/4 teaspoon black pepper (1.25g)

**Prep. time:** 5 min | **Total time:** 35 min | **Servings:** 2

## Directions

1. Preheat your oven to 200°C (180°C fan) or Gas Mark 6.
2. Drain and rinse the chickpeas thoroughly under cold water. Pat the chickpeas dry using a clean tea towel or kitchen paper. Removing excess moisture helps them roast properly.
3. In a medium bowl, combine the chickpeas with olive oil, paprika, ground cumin, garlic powder, onion powder, sea salt, and black pepper. Toss until the chickpeas are evenly coated with the spices and oil.
4. Spread the seasoned chickpeas in a single layer on a baking tray. Roast in the preheated oven for 25-30 minutes, shaking the tray halfway through to ensure even cooking. The chickpeas are done when they are golden brown and crispy.
5. Remove the tray from the oven and let the chickpeas cool for a few minutes before serving. Serve immediately for the best crunch, or store in an airtight container for up to 2 days.

---

Nutritional value (per serving):

Calories – 228.2 kcal
Protein – 8g
Carbohydrates – 27g
Sugars – 4.6g
Fibre – 7.6g
Fat – 9.8g
Saturated Fat – 1.3g

**Tips for Glycaemic Control:** Chickpeas have a low glycaemic index and are high in fibre and protein, making them an excellent snack choice for blood sugar management.

**Serving Suggestions:** Pair these roasted chickpeas with a small serving of fresh vegetable sticks such as cucumber, celery, or carrot for added fibre and nutrients. Use these roasted chickpeas as a crunchy topping for salads.

**Gluten-Free:** This recipe is naturally gluten-free.

**Vegan:** This recipe is naturally vegan.

# Celery Sticks with Cottage Cheese

### Ingredients

- 4 large celery sticks (200g)
- 150g cottage cheese (low-fat)
- 1 tablespoon fresh chives, finely chopped (5g)
- 1 teaspoon fresh parsley, finely chopped (2g)
- 1/4 teaspoon black pepper (1.25g)
- 1/4 teaspoon paprika (1.25g)

**Prep. time:** 10 min | **Total time:** 10 min | **Servings:** 2

### Directions

1. Wash the celery sticks thoroughly under cold running water. Cut each celery stick into 2-3 pieces, depending on length, to create manageable snack-sized portions.
2. In a medium bowl, combine the cottage cheese, chopped chives, and parsley. Add black pepper and paprika to the mixture. Mix well until all ingredients are evenly distributed.
3. Spoon the cottage cheese mixture into the hollow of each celery stick piece, distributing it evenly.
4. Arrange the filled celery sticks on a plate and serve immediately.

---

Nutritional value (per serving):

Calories – 80 kcal
Protein – 10.4 g
Carbohydrates – 6g
Sugars – 3.62g
Fibre – 2.14g
Fat – 1.6g
Saturated Fat – 0.82g

**Tips for Glycaemic Control:** Celery is a low-glycaemic, low- calorie vegetable that adds a satisfying crunch to this snack without affecting blood sugar levels.

**Serving Suggestions:** Pair this snack with a handful of nuts or a small piece of fruit for a more balanced and filling snack option. Arrange these stuffed celery sticks on a platter for a healthy and visually appealing appetizer at gatherings.

**Gluten-Free:** This recipe is naturally gluten-free.

**Vegan:** Replace cottage cheese with a vegan cream cheese alternative to make this snack vegan-friendly.

# Baked Kale Chips with Sea Salt

## Ingredients

- 100g kale leaves (stems removed, torn into bite-sized pieces)
- 1 tablespoon olive oil (15ml)
- 1/2 teaspoon sea salt (2.5g)
- 1/4 teaspoon garlic powder (1.25g)
- 1/4 teaspoon paprika (1.25g)

**Prep. time:** 10 min | **Total time:** 30 min | **Servings:** 2

## Directions

1. Preheat your oven to 150°C (300°F). Line a baking tray with parchment paper.
2. Wash the kale leaves thoroughly and dry them completely. It is crucial that the kale is dry to ensure it bakes to a crisp texture. Tear the kale into bite-sized pieces, removing any tough stems.
3. In a large bowl, toss the kale pieces with olive oil, ensuring they are evenly coated. Sprinkle the sea salt, garlic powder, and paprika over the kale. Toss again to distribute the seasoning evenly.
4. Spread the seasoned kale pieces in a single layer on the lined baking tray. Bake in the preheated oven for 15-20 minutes, turning halfway through, until the kale is crisp but not burnt. Keep an eye on them towards the end of the baking time to prevent over cooking.
5. Allow the kale chips to cool slightly before serving. Enjoy them fresh for the best texture and flavour.

Nutritional value (per serving):

Calories – 94.2 kcal
Protein – 2.2g
Carbohydrates – 4.7g
Sugars – 0.7g
Fibre – 1.3g
Fat – 7.4g
Saturated Fat – 1.02g

**Tips for Glycaemic Control:** Kale is a low-glycaemic, high-fibre vegetable that helps maintain stable blood sugar levels.

**Serving Suggestions:** Pair these kale chips with a small portion of nuts or a slice of cheese for a balanced snack. Serve alongside a lean protein, such as grilled chicken or fish, for a nutritious meal.

**Gluten-Free:** This recipe is naturally gluten-free.

**Vegan:** This recipe is naturally vegan.

# Mixed Nuts and Dried Unsweetened Berries

## Ingredients

- 50g mixed nuts (almonds, walnuts, cashews, etc.)
- 30g dried unsweetened berries (such as cranberries, blueberries, or goji berries)
- 1/2 teaspoon ground cinnamon (optional)
- Pinch of sea salt (optional)

**Prep. time:** 5 min | **Total time:** 5 min | **Servings:** 2

## Directions

1. If the nuts are not already chopped or mixed, measure out 50g of mixed nuts. You can use a combination of almonds, walnuts, cashews, or any other nuts you prefer.
2. Combine the mixed nuts with 30g of dried unsweetened berries in a bowl.
3. If desired, add a pinch of sea salt and 1/2 teaspoon of ground cinnamon to the nuts and berries mixture. Toss gently to coat evenly.
4. Divide the mixed nuts and dried berries into two equal portions and serve immediately.

---

Nutritional value (per serving):

Calories – 210.8 kcal
Protein – 5g
Carbohydrates – 16.2g
Sugars – 10g
Fibre – 3.1g
Fat – 14g
Saturated Fat – 1.5g

**Tips for Glycaemic Control:** Dried unsweetened berries, such as cranberries or blueberries, provide natural sweetness and fibre without the added sugars found in sweetened dried fruits.

**Serving Suggestions:** Enjoy as a standalone snack or pair with a small piece of cheese or a serving of Greek yogurt for added protein. Pack in a small container for a convenient snack during travel or between meals.

**Gluten-Free:** This recipe is naturally gluten-free.

**Vegan:** This recipe is naturally vegan.

# Edamame with a Sprinkle of Sea Salt

## Ingredients

- 200g frozen edamame in pods
- 1 teaspoon sea salt
  Optional for enhanced flavour: 1 teaspoon toasted sesame seeds,
- 1/2 teaspoon chilli flakes, or a squeeze of fresh lemon juice

**Prep. time:** 5 min

**Total time:** 10 min

**Servings:** 2

## Directions

1. Bring a large pot of water to a boil. Add the frozen edamame to the boiling water. Cook for 3- 5 minutes, or until the edamame pods are tender and bright green. Drain the edamame in a colander and rinse under cold water to stop the cooking process.
2. Transfer the drained edamame to a large bowl. Sprinkle the sea salt over the edamame and toss to evenly distribute the salt. For additional flavour, you can add toasted sesame seeds, chilli flakes, or a squeeze of fresh lemon juice.

---

Nutritional value (per serving) without optional ingredients:

Calories – 129 kcal
Protein – 11g
Carbohydrates – 10g
Sugars – 2g
Fibre – 5g
Fat – 5g
Saturated Fat – 0.5g

---

**Tips for Glycaemic Control:** Ensure that any additional seasonings, such as sesame seeds or chilli flakes, do not contain added sugars.

**Serving Suggestions:** Serve the edamame as a snack or appetiser. It pairs well with a variety of main dishes, particularly Asian-inspired meals. For a more substantial snack, pair with a small portion of mixed nuts or a few slices of avocado.

**Gluten-Free:** This recipe is naturally gluten-free.

**Vegan:** This recipe is naturally vegan.

# Cherry Tomatoes and Mozzarella Balls

## Ingredients

- 200g cherry tomatoes
- 150g mozzarella balls (mini mozzarella or bocconcini)
- 1 tablespoon extra-virgin olive oil
- 1 tablespoon balsamic vinegar (optional)
- Fresh basil leaves, torn
- Salt and black pepper, to taste

**Prep. time:** 10 min
**Total time:** 10 min
**Servings:** 2

## Directions

1. Rinse 200g of cherry tomatoes under cold water. Pat them dry with a paper towel. Drain 150g of mozzarella balls (mini mozzarella or bocconcini) if they are stored in liquid.
2. On a serving plate, arrange the cherry tomatoes and mozzarella balls. Scatter torn fresh basil leaves over the tomatoes and mozzarella.
3. Drizzle 1 tablespoon of extra virgin olive oil evenly over the tomatoes and mozzarella. Optionally, add 1 tablespoon of balsamic vinegar for extra flavour.
4. Sprinkle with salt and black pepper to taste. Serve immediately and enjoy!

Nutritional value (per serving) without optional ingredients:

Calories – 269 kcal (without vinegar) or 277 kcal (with vinegar)
Protein – 15g
Carbohydrates – 5g or 7g
Sugars – 4g or 6g
Fibre – 1g
Fat – 21g
Saturated Fat - 10g

**Tips for Glycaemic Control:** Cherry tomatoes are low in carbohydrates and have a low glycaemic index, providing vitamins and antioxidants.

**Serving Suggestions:** Enjoy as a light snack between meals. Include in a mixed green salad for a more substantial dish.

**Gluten-Free:** This recipe is naturally gluten-free.

**Vegan:** Substitute mozzarella balls with vegan mozzarella or tofu cubes for a dairy-free option.

# Bell Pepper Slices with Guacamole

## Ingredients

- 1 large red bell pepper
- 1 large yellow bell pepper
- 1 large green bell pepper
- 2 ripe avocados
- 1 small tomato, diced
- 1/2 small red onion, finely chopped
- 1 clove garlic, minced
- Juice of 1 lime
- 1 tablespoon chopped fresh coriander
- Salt and black pepper, to taste

**Prep. time:** 15 min | **Total time:** 15 min | **Servings:** 2

## Directions

1. Rinse and dry the bell peppers. Cut each pepper in half, remove the seeds and stem, then slice each half into thin strips.
2. Cut the avocados in half, remove the pits, and scoop the flesh into a bowl. Mash the avocado with a fork until smooth or slightly chunky, depending on preference. Add diced tomato, finely chopped red onion, minced garlic, lime juice, and chopped coriander to the mashed avocado. Mix well to combine. Season with salt and black pepper to taste. Adjust lime juice or salt as needed.
3. Arrange the bell pepper slices on a serving plate. Spoon the guacamole into a small bowl and place it in the centre of the plate or serve alongside the bell pepper slices.
4. Serve immediately and enjoy!

Nutritional value (per serving):

Calories – 338 kcal
Protein – 6g
Carbohydrates – 29g
Sugars – 13g
Fibre – 15g
Fat – 22g
Saturated Fat – 3g

**Tips for Glycaemic Control:** Avocados are high in healthy fats and fibre, which help stabilise blood sugar levels. Avoid adding sugar or high-carb ingredients to maintain low glycaemic index.

**Serving Suggestions:** Perfect for a midday snack to keep blood sugar levels stable. Pair with a side salad for a light and satisfying meal.

**Gluten-Free:** This recipe is naturally gluten-free.

**Vegan:** Suitable for vegan diets.

# 6 – DELIGHTFUL DESSERTS

## Sugar Alternatives: Using Sweeteners Wisely

In the realm of diabetic-friendly desserts, the quest for sweetness without compromising blood sugar levels is paramount. Traditional sugars can cause spikes in blood glucose, making it essential for diabetics to seek out suitable alternatives that provide the desired sweetness while maintaining glycaemic control.

### The Need for Sugar Alternatives

For individuals managing diabetes, controlling carbohydrate intake is crucial. Sugars, particularly refined ones, are high on the glycaemic index (GI), meaning they cause rapid increases in blood glucose levels. By replacing these with low-GI alternatives, it is possible to enjoy sweet treats without the adverse effects on blood sugar. However, not all sugar substitutes are created equal. Understanding their properties, benefits, and potential drawbacks is essential for making informed choices.

### Types of Sugar Alternatives

1. Natural Sweeteners:
   - Stevia: Derived from the leaves of the Stevia rebaudiana plant, stevia is a popular natural sweetener. It is extremely sweet, often requiring only a small amount to achieve the desired level of sweetness. Stevia has a negligible effect on blood glucose levels and is calorie-free.
   - Monk Fruit: Also known as Luo Han Guo, monk fruit extract is another natural, zero-calorie sweetener. It is significantly sweeter than sugar and does not impact blood glucose levels.
   - Erythritol: This sugar alcohol occurs naturally in some fruits and fermented foods. It has about 70% of the sweetness of sugar and is almost calorie-free. Erythritol does not raise blood sugar or insulin levels.
2. Artificial Sweeteners:
   - Aspartame: Commonly found in diet sodas and sugar-free products, aspartame is much sweeter than sugar, so only a small amount is needed. It is low-calorie and does not affect blood glucose levels.
   - Sucralose: Sucralose is another widely used artificial sweetener. It is heat-stable, making it suitable for baking and cooking.
3. Sugar Alcohols:
   - Xylitol: While xylitol has a similar sweetness level to sugar, it contains fewer calories and has a lower glycaemic index. It can be found in many sugar-free gums and dental products.
   - Sorbitol: Commonly used in sugar-free candies and baked goods, sorbitol has about half the sweetness of sugar and is low in calories. However, it can have a laxative effect if consumed in large quantities.

# **Tips for Using Sweeteners Wisely**

1. Understand Sweetness Levels:

Each sweetener varies in sweetness intensity compared to sugar. For example, stevia and monk fruit are much sweeter than sugar, so adjust the quantities accordingly to avoid over-sweetening your desserts.

2. Consider Taste and Aftertaste:

Some sweeteners, particularly stevia, can have a distinct aftertaste. Experiment with combinations of sweeteners to find a balance that suits your palate.

3. Use in Moderation:

While these alternatives can help manage blood sugar levels, it is important to use them in moderation. Overconsumption of certain sweeteners, like sugar alcohols, can cause digestive discomfort.

4. Incorporate Natural Flavours:

Enhance the sweetness and flavour of your desserts by incorporating natural ingredients like vanilla extract, cinnamon, and fresh fruits. These can reduce the need for additional sweeteners.

5. Heat Stability:

Some sweeteners, like aspartame, may lose their sweetness when exposed to high temperatures. Choose heat-stable options such as sucralose or erythritol for baking.

Incorporating sugar alternatives into your diet can significantly enhance your ability to enjoy sweet treats without compromising your health. By understanding the properties and appropriate uses of these sweeteners, you can make informed decisions that align with your dietary needs. Always consult with a healthcare professional or a registered dietitian to tailor these recommendations to your individual health requirements. With the right knowledge and a bit of creativity, you can indulge in delightful desserts that support your journey towards optimal glycaemic control and overall well-being.

# Dark Chocolate Avocado Mousse

### Ingredients

- 1 ripe avocado (approximately 150g)
- 30g unsweetened dark cocoa powder (at least 70% cocoa)
- 60ml unsweetened almond milk (or any other plant-based milk)
- 1-2 tablespoons erythritol or stevia (adjust to taste)
- 1 teaspoon vanilla extract
- A pinch of sea salt

**Prep. time:** 10 min | **Total time:** 10 min | **Servings:** 2

### Directions

1. Cut the avocado in half, remove the pit, and scoop the flesh into a blender or food processor.
2. Add the dark cocoa powder, almond milk, erythritol or stevia, vanilla extract, and sea salt to the blender.
3. Blend all the ingredients until you get a smooth and creamy texture. You may need to stop and scrape down the sides of the blender a few times to ensure everything is well combined.
4. Taste the mousse and adjust the sweetness by adding a little more erythritol or stevia if necessary. Blend again briefly to mix.
5. Spoon the mousse into serving bowls. You can eat it immediately or chill it in the refrigerator for about 30 minutes if you prefer a firmer texture.

Nutritional value (per serving):

Calories – 215.7 kcal
Protein – 5.2g
Carbohydrates – 16.1g
Sugars – 0.85g
Fibre – 9.25g
Fat – 14.5g
Saturated Fat – 3.3g

**Tips for Enhancing Flavour:** Sprinkle a pinch of cinnamon or nutmeg into the mousse for a warm, spicy note. Add a teaspoon of freshly grated orange zest to the mixture before blending for a bright, citrusy flavour. Garnish with fresh mint leaves for a refreshing finish.

**Serving Suggestions:** Top with fresh berries (like raspberries or strawberries) for an additional burst of flavour and antioxidants. Add a sprinkle of chopped nuts or seeds for a crunchy contrast.

**Nut-Free:** Substitute almond milk with coconut milk or oat milk if you have nut allergies.

**Vegan:** Ensure all ingredients, including sweeteners, are vegan.

# Baked Apple with Cinnamon and Walnuts

## Ingredients

- 2 medium-sized apples (approximately 150g each), such as Granny Smith or Braeburn
- 30g chopped walnuts
- 1 teaspoon ground cinnamon
- 1 tablespoon melted coconut oil (or olive oil)
- 1 teaspoon vanilla extract
- 1 tablespoon erythritol or stevia (optional, adjust to taste)
- 2 tablespoons water

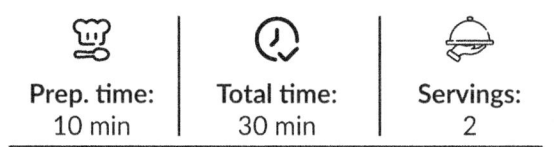

**Prep. time:** 10 min | **Total time:** 30 min | **Servings:** 2

## Directions

1. Preheat your oven to 180°C (350°F, Gas Mark 4).
2. Wash and core the apples, leaving the bottom intact to create a well for the filling. If you prefer, you can also peel the apples, but leaving the skin on retains more fibre.
3. In a small bowl, mix the chopped walnuts, ground cinnamon, melted coconut oil, vanilla extract, and erythritol or stevia (if using). Place the apples in a baking dish. Divide the walnut mixture evenly between the two apples, stuffing it into the core wells.
4. Pour the water into the bottom of the baking dish to help steam the apples during baking, keeping them moist. Cover the baking dish with foil and bake in the preheated oven for 20 minutes. Remove the foil and bake for an additional 5-10 minutes, or until the apples are tender and the filling is golden.
5. Allow the apples to cool slightly before serving. They can be enjoyed warm or at room temperature.

---

Nutritional value (per serving):

Calories – 270 kcal
Protein – 2.65g
Carbohydrates – 26.25g
Sugars – 15.35g
Fibre – 5.65g
Fat – 17.15g
Saturated Fat – 6.9g

**Tips for Enhancing Flavour:** Add a pinch of nutmeg or ground ginger to the walnut mixture for extra warmth and complexity. If the apples are naturally sweet, you may not need the additional erythritol or stevia.

**Serving Suggestions:** Serve with a dollop of Greek yogurt for added protein and creaminess. Pair with a boiled egg or a slice of whole-grain toast for a balanced breakfast.

**Nut-Free:** Replace walnuts with sunflower seeds or pumpkin seeds.

**Vegan:** This recipe is naturally vegan.

# Chia Seed Pudding with Coconut Milk

## Ingredients

- 60g chia seeds
- 400ml coconut milk (unsweetened, full fat)
- 1 teaspoon vanilla extract
- 1 tablespoon erythritol or stevia (optional, adjust to taste)
- Fresh berries or a sprinkle of cinnamon for topping (optional)

**Prep. time:** 5 min | **Total time:** 4h 5 min | **Servings:** 2

## Directions

1. In a medium-sized bowl, combine the chia seeds, coconut milk, vanilla extract, and erythritol or stevia (if using). Stir well to ensure the chia seeds are evenly distributed and not clumping.
2. Cover the bowl and refrigerate for at least 4 hours, or preferably overnight. This allows the chia seeds to absorb the liquid and form a pudding-like consistency.
3. Before serving, give the pudding a good stir to make sure the chia seeds are evenly distributed. Divide the mixture into two serving bowls.
4. Top with fresh berries or a sprinkle of cinnamon, if desired. These add a burst of flavour and additional nutrients without significantly affecting blood sugar levels.

---

Nutritional value (per serving):

Calories – 314 kcal
Protein – 7g
Carbohydrates – 19.75g
Sugars – 0g
Fibre – 12g
Fat – 23g
Saturated Fat – 12.9g

---

**Tips for Enhancing Flavour:** Add a tablespoon of cocoa powder for a chocolate version or mix in some mashed banana for natural sweetness (adjust carbohydrate content accordingly).

**Serving Suggestions:** Pair with a hard-boiled egg or a slice of whole-grain toast for a balanced breakfast. Enjoy as a mid-morning or afternoon snack to keep energy levels stable.

**Nut-Free:** This recipe is naturally nut-free, but always check for potential cross-contamination if you have severe allergies.

**Vegan:** This recipe is naturally vegan.

# Sugar-Free Lemon Cheesecake Bites

## Ingredients

- 100g cream cheese (full fat, softened)
- 50g Greek yoghurt (unsweetened)
- 1 tablespoon fresh lemon juice
- 1 teaspoon lemon zest
- 1 tablespoon erythritol or stevia (adjust to taste)
- 1 teaspoon vanilla extract
- 2 digestive biscuits (no sugar, gluten-free if needed)
- 1 tablespoon unsalted butter, melted

**Prep. time:** 15 min | **Total time:** 1 h 15 min | **Servings:** 2

## Directions

1. Crush the digestive biscuits into fine crumbs.
2. Mix the crumbs with the melted butter until well combined. Divide the mixture evenly into silicone mini muffin cups or a small baking dish, pressing down firmly to form the base.
3. In a mixing bowl, combine the softened cream cheese, Greek yoghurt, lemon juice, lemon zest, erythritol or stevia, and vanilla extract. Beat until smooth and creamy.
4. Spoon the cheesecake mixture over the prepared bases, smoothing the tops with the back of a spoon. Refrigerate for at least 1 hour, or until set.
5. Carefully remove the cheesecake bites from the moulds or cut into squares if using a baking dish. Serve chilled.

Nutritional value (per serving):

Calories – 329.6 kcal
Protein – 6.5g
Carbohydrates – 17.95g
Sugars – 5.25g
Fibre – 1.1g
Fat – 25.75g
Saturated Fat – 14.65g

**Tips for Enhancing Flavour:** Swap lemon with lime for a different citrus profile.

**Serving Suggestions:** Garnish with fresh berries or a small sprig of mint. Pair with a cup of herbal tea for a relaxing snack.

**Gluten-Free:** Ensure the digestive biscuits are gluten-free.

**Vegan:** Use a plant-based cream cheese and yoghurt alternative.

# Raspberry Yoghurt Popsicles

### Ingredients

- 150g fresh or frozen raspberries (unsweetened)
- 200g Greek yoghurt (unsweetened)
- 1 tablespoon erythritol or stevia (adjust to taste)
- 1 teaspoon vanilla extract
- 50ml water

**Prep. time:** 10 min
**Total time:** 4h 10 min
**Servings:** 2

### Directions

1. If using frozen raspberries, let them thaw slightly. Blend the raspberries with 50ml of water until smooth. If desired, strain the mixture to remove seeds for a smoother texture.
2. In a mixing bowl, combine the Greek yoghurt, erythritol or stevia, and vanilla extract. Mix until the sweetener is fully dissolved, and the yoghurt is smooth.
3. In popsicle moulds, alternate layers of the raspberry puree and the yoghurt mixture. Use a skewer or knife to gently swirl the layers together for a marbled effect.
4. Insert popsicle sticks into the moulds. Freeze for at least 4 hours, or until completely solid.
5. To remove the popsicles from the moulds, run warm water over the outside of the moulds for a few seconds. Serve immediately.

---

Nutritional value (per serving):

Calories – 120.3 kcal
Protein – 10.75g
Carbohydrates – 14.15g
Sugars – 6.3g
Fibre – 4.9g
Fat – 2.3g
Saturated Fat – 1.2g

---

**Tips for Enhancing Flavour:** Add a few fresh mint leaves to the raspberry puree before blending for a refreshing twist. Substitute raspberries with other low-glycaemic fruits like strawberries or blueberries.

**Serving Suggestions:** Sprinkle with finely chopped nuts or seeds before freezing for added texture. Serve alongside a small portion of mixed nuts for a more substantial snack.

**Gluten-Free:** Ensure any added flavourings or sweeteners are gluten-free.

**Vegan:** Use a plant-based yoghurt alternative, such as almond or coconut yoghurt.

# Almond Flour Chocolate Chip Cookie

## Ingredients

- 100g almond flour
- 1/4 teaspoon baking powder
- 1/8 teaspoon sea salt
- 2 tablespoons coconut oil, melted
- 2 tablespoons erythritol or stevia (adjust to taste)
- 1 teaspoon vanilla extract
- 1 large egg
- 50g dark chocolate chips (at least 70% cocoa, sugar-free if available)

**Prep. time:** 15 min | **Total time:** 30 min | **Servings:** 2

## Directions

1. Preheat your oven to 175°C (350°F) and line a baking tray with parchment paper.
2. In a medium bowl, combine the almond flour, baking powder, and sea salt. Mix well to ensure even distribution.
3. In a separate bowl, whisk together the melted coconut oil, erythritol or stevia, vanilla extract, and egg until well combined.
4. Gradually add the dry ingredients to the wet mixture, stirring until a dough forms. Fold in the dark chocolate chips until evenly distributed.
5. Scoop out tablespoon-sized portions of dough and roll them into balls. Place them on the prepared baking tray, leaving enough space between each ball. Gently flatten each ball with the palm of your hand to form cookie shapes.
6. Bake in the preheated oven for 12-15 minutes, or until the edges of the cookies are golden brown. Allow the cookies to cool on the baking tray for a few minutes before transferring them to a wire rack to cool completely.

Nutritional value (per serving):

Calories – 643.2 kcal
Protein – 16.2g
Carbohydrates – 25.8g
Sugars – 2.15g
Fibre – 11.35g
Fat – 52.8g
Saturated Fat – 21.2g

**Tips for Enhancing Flavour:** Add a pinch of cinnamon or a drop of almond extract to the dough for additional flavour without adding extra sugar. For added crunch, mix in a tablespoon of chopped nuts such as walnuts or pecans.

**Serving Suggestions:** Serve with a cup of unsweetened almond milk or herbal tea for a comforting snack. Enjoy as a dessert following a balanced meal.

**Different Add-ins:** Substitute dark chocolate chips with unsweetened dried cranberries or blueberries for a fruity twist.

**Vegan:** Replace the egg with a flax egg (1 tablespoon ground flaxseed mixed with 3 tablespoons water, let sit for 5 minutes).

# Berry Crumble with Oats and Almonds

## Ingredients

**For the Filling:**
- 150g mixed berries (e.g., blueberries, raspberries, and strawberries)
- 1 tablespoon lemon juice
- 1 teaspoon vanilla extract
- 1 tablespoon erythritol or stevia (adjust to taste)

**For the Crumble Topping:**
- 40g rolled oats
- 30g almond flour
- 2 tablespoons chopped almonds
- 1 tablespoon coconut oil, melted
- 1 tablespoon erythritol or stevia (adjust to taste)
- 1/2 teaspoon ground cinnamon
- A pinch of sea salt

**Prep. time:** 10 min | **Total time:** 30 min | **Servings:** 2

## Directions

1. Preheat your oven to 180°C (350°F).
2. In a medium bowl, combine the mixed berries, lemon juice, vanilla extract, and 1 tablespoon of erythritol or stevia. Toss gently to coat the berries evenly. Divide the mixture between two small ovenproof dishes.
3. In another bowl, mix the rolled oats, almond flour, chopped almonds, melted coconut oil, 1 tablespoon of erythritol or stevia, ground cinnamon, and a pinch of sea salt until well combined.
4. Sprinkle the crumble topping evenly over the berry mixture in each dish.
5. Place the dishes on a baking tray and bake in the preheated oven for 20 minutes, or until the topping is golden brown and the berries are bubbling.
6. Allow the crumbles to cool for a few minutes before serving. Enjoy warm.

**Nutritional value (per serving):**

Calories – 323 kcal
Protein – 8.05g
Carbohydrates – 27.35g
Sugars – 6.4g
Fibre – 8.1g
Fat – 20.15g
Saturated Fat – 7.05g

**Tips for Enhancing Flavour:** Add a pinch of nutmeg or cardamom to the crumble topping for a warm, spicy flavour.

**Serving Suggestions:** Enjoy as a light dessert following a balanced meal, with a dollop of Greek yogurt on the side.

**Gluten-Free:** Ensure that the oats used are certified gluten-free to cater to gluten-intolerant individuals.

**Vegan:** This recipe is already vegan but ensure the sweeteners you use are also vegan-friendly.

# Pumpkin Spice Energy Balls

## Ingredients

- 100g pumpkin puree
- 50g almond flour
- 30g rolled oats
- 25g chopped walnuts
- 2 tablespoons chia seeds
- 2 tablespoons unsweetened shredded coconut
- 1 teaspoon vanilla extract
- 1 teaspoon ground cinnamon
- 1/2 teaspoon ground ginger
- 1/4 teaspoon ground nutmeg
- A pinch of salt

**Prep. time:** 15 min | **Total time:** 45 min | **Servings:** 2

## Directions

1. In a mixing bowl, combine the pumpkin puree, almond flour, rolled oats, chopped walnuts, chia seeds, unsweetened shredded coconut, vanilla extract, ground cinnamon, ground ginger, ground nutmeg, and a pinch of salt. Mix well until all ingredients are evenly combined.
2. Take small portions of the mixture and roll them into balls about 1-inch in diameter. Place each ball on a plate or baking sheet lined with parchment paper.
3. Chill the energy balls in the refrigerator for about 30 minutes to firm them up.
4. Once chilled (if desired), serve immediately or store in an airtight container in the refrigerator for up to one week.

Nutritional value (per serving):

Calories – 434 kcal
Protein – 12.6g
Carbohydrates – 27.5g
Sugars – 3.5g
Fibre – 12.3g
Fat – 30.4g
Saturated Fat – 5.5g

**Tips for Enhancing Flavour:** Adjust the amount of cinnamon, ginger, and nutmeg to suit your taste preferences.

**Serving Suggestions:** Enjoy these energy balls as a mid-morning or afternoon snack with a cup of herbal tea or a glass of unsweetened almond milk. They also make a great pre- or post-workout snack due to their balanced macronutrient profile.

**Gluten-Free:** Confirm oats are certified gluten-free to cater to gluten-intolerant individuals.

**Vegan:** This recipe is naturally vegan.

# Coconut Macaroons with Dark Chocolate Drizzle

## Ingredients

- 100g unsweetened shredded coconut
- 50g almond flour
- 50g egg whites (about 2 large eggs)
- 40g erythritol (or preferred sugar substitute)
- 30ml coconut oil, melted
- 1/2 teaspoon vanilla extract
- 50g dark chocolate (70% cocoa or higher), for drizzling

**Prep. time:** 15 min | **Total time:** 40 min | **Servings:** 2

## Directions

1. Preheat your oven to 160°C (325°F) and line a baking sheet with parchment paper.
2. In a mixing bowl, combine the unsweetened shredded coconut, almond flour, erythritol, melted coconut oil, and vanilla extract. Mix well until thoroughly combined.
3. In a separate bowl, whisk the egg whites until they form stiff peaks. Gently fold the whipped egg whites into the coconut mixture until evenly incorporated.
4. Using a spoon or your hands, shape the mixture into 8 small macaroons and place them on the lined baking sheet, evenly spaced.
5. Bake in the preheated oven for 15 minutes, or until the macaroons are golden brown on the edges. Remove from the oven and allow them to cool completely on a wire rack.
6. While the macaroons are cooling, melt the dark chocolate in a heatproof bowl over simmering water or in the microwave in short bursts, stirring frequently until smooth.
7. Once the macaroons have cooled, drizzle the melted dark chocolate over the tops of the macaroons using a spoon or a piping bag.
8. Allow the chocolate drizzle to set at room temperature or in the refrigerator before serving.

---

Nutritional value (per serving):

Calories – 796.3 kcal
Protein – 13.75g
Carbohydrates – 31.75g
Sugars – 9.05g
Fibre – 15.15g
Fat – 68.25g
Saturated Fat – 48.15g

**Tips for Enhancing Flavour:** Enjoy these Coconut Macaroons as a delightful snack with a cup of herbal tea or coffee. They also make a fantastic addition to a dessert platter for special occasions or afternoon tea.

**Serving Suggestions:** Enjoy these energy balls as a mid-morning or afternoon snack with a cup of herbal tea or a glass of unsweetened almond milk. They also make a great pre- or post-workout snack due to their balanced macronutrient profile.

**Gluten-Free:** Ensure all ingredients are certified gluten-free to cater to gluten- intolerant individuals.

**Vegan:** Substitute egg whites with aquafaba (chickpea brine) or a commercial egg replacer for a vegan-friendly option.

# Pears Poached in Red Wine with a Cinnamon Stick

## Ingredients

- 2 medium pears, ripe but firm
- 250ml red wine (use a dry red wine such as Merlot or Cabernet Sauvignon)
- 250ml water
- 50g erythritol (or preferred sugar substitute)
- 1 cinnamon stick
- Zest of 1 orange (optional)
- Greek yogurt or whipped cream, for serving (optional)

**Prep. time:** 10 min | **Total time:** 40 min | **Servings:** 2

## Directions

1. Peel the pears, leaving the stems intact. Optionally, rub the peeled pears with lemon juice to prevent browning.
2. In a medium saucepan, combine the red wine, water, erythritol, cinnamon stick, and orange zest (if using). Bring to a gentle simmer over medium heat, stirring occasionally until the erythritol dissolves.
3. Carefully add the pears to the poaching liquid, ensuring they are submerged. Reduce the heat to low and simmer gently for about 20-30 minutes, or until the pears are tender when pierced with a fork. Turn the pears occasionally for even cooking.
4. Once tender, remove the pears from the poaching liquid and set aside to cool slightly. Optionally, strain the poaching liquid to remove the cinnamon stick and orange zest.
5. Increase the heat to medium-high and simmer the poaching liquid until it reduces and thickens slightly, about 10-15 minutes. This can be drizzled over the pears for added flavour.
6. Serve the pears warm or chilled, drizzled with a little of the reduced poaching liquid if desired. Optionally, serve with a dollop of Greek yogurt or whipped cream for added richness.

Nutritional value (per serving) without optional ingredients:

Calories – 135.5 kcal
Protein – 0.55g
Carbohydrates – 33g
Sugars – 19g
Fibre – 6.65g
Fat – 0.25g
Saturated Fat – 0.05g

**Tips for Enhancing Flavour:** Experiment with adding a star anise or a few cloves to the poaching liquid for additional aromatic notes.

**Serving Suggestions:** Enjoy these Pears Poached in Red Wine as a sophisticated snack or dessert option.

**Gluten-Free:** Naturally, glutenfree; ensure all ingredients are certified gluten-free.

**Vegan:** Substitute erythritol with a vegan-friendly sweetener and serve with dairy-free yogurt or whipped coconut cream.

# 7 - MEAL PLANNING AND PREP

## Weekly Meal Plans: Sample Plans for Beginners

Planning meals ahead can simplify your week and ensure you stick to your dietary goals, especially when managing diabetes. Below are sample meal plans featuring recipes from earlier chapters.

|  | Monday | Tuesday | Wednesday | Thursday | Friday | Saturday | Sunday |
| --- | --- | --- | --- | --- | --- | --- | --- |
| **Breakfast** | Scrambled Tofu with Vegetables (Chapter 2, Recipe 3) | Chia Seed Pudding with Almond Milk and Berries (Chapter 2, Recipe 2) | Oatmeal with Flaxseeds and Blueberries (Chapter 2, Recipe 9) | Whole Grain Toast with Smashed Avocado and Cherry Tomatoes (Chapter 2, Recipe 4) | Avocado and Spinach Smoothie (Chapter 2, Recipe 1) | Smoked Salmon and Cucumber Roll-Ups (Chapter 2, Recipe 10) | Cottage Cheese and Berry Parfait (Chapter 2, Recipe 7) |
| **Snack** | Greek Yogurt with Nuts and Fresh Fruit (Chapter 2, Recipe 5) | Hummus with Cucumber and Carrot Sticks (Chapter 5, Recipe 1) | Greek Yogurt with Walnuts and Fresh Berries (Chapter 2, Recipe 5) | Roasted Chickpeas with Paprika (Chapter 5, Recipe 4) | Apple Slices with Almond Butter (Chapter 5, Recipe 2) | Greek Yogurt with Nuts and Fresh Fruit (Chapter 2, Recipe 5) | Apple Slices with Almond Butter (Chapter 5, Recipe 2) |
| **Lunch** | Grilled Chicken Salad with Mixed Greens and Lemon Vinaigrette (Chapter 3, Recipe 1) | Turkey and Avocado Lettuce Wraps (Chapter 3, Recipe 3) | Chickpea and Tuna Salad with Lemon Vinaigrette (Chapter 3, Recipe 6) | Spinach and Mushroom Stuffed Bell Peppers (Chapter 3, Recipe 5) | Quinoa and Black Bean Salad with Lime Dressing (Chapter 3, Recipe 2) | Lentil and Vegetable Soup (Chapter 3, Recipe 4) | Zucchini Noodles with Pesto and Cherry Tomatoes (Chapter 3, Recipe 8) |
| **Snack** | Apple Slices with Almond Butter (Chapter 5, Recipe 2) | Mixed Nuts and Dried Unsweetened Berries (Chapter 5, Recipe 7) | Edamame with a Sprinkle of Sea Salt (Chapter 5, Recipe 8) | Celery Sticks with Cottage Cheese (Chapter 5, Recipe 5) | Baked Kale Chips with Sea Salt (Chapter 5, Recipe 6) | Mixed Nuts and Dried Unsweetened Berries (Chapter 5, Recipe 7) | Roasted Chickpeas with Paprika (Chapter 5, Recipe 4) |

| Dinner | Baked Salmon with Asparagus and Quinoa (Chapter 4, Recipe 1) | Vegetable Curry with Cauliflower Rice (Chapter 4, Recipe 6) | Stir-Fried Tofu with Mixed Vegetables (Chapter 4, Recipe 3) | Lean Beef Stir-Fry with Bell Peppers and Snow Peas (Chapter 4, Recipe 7) | Stuffed Portobello Mush-rooms with Spinach and Cheese (Chapter 4, Recipe 9) | Herb-Crusted Pork Tenderloin with Green Beans (Chapter 4, Recipe 8) | Spaghetti Squash with Marinara and Turkey Meat Sauce (Chapter 4, Recipe 10) |
|---|---|---|---|---|---|---|---|

# Shopping List

### Produce:

- Spinach
- Tomatoes
- Bell peppers (assorted colours)
- Avocados
- Mixed greens (for salads)
- Fresh berries (e.g., strawberries, blueberries)
- Lemons
- Cucumber
- Carrots
- Apples
- Kale
- Celery
- Portobello mushrooms
- Zucchini
- Cherry tomatoes
- Green beans
- Garlic
- Onion
- Cauliflower
- Basil

### Meat, Poultry, and Fish:

- Salmon fillets
- Chicken breast (skinless)
- Turkey breast (skinless)
- Pork tenderloin
- Lean beef (for stir-fry)
- Smoked salmon
- Turkey meat (lean for spaghetti sauce)

### Dairy and Alternatives:

- Greek yogurt (plain, unsweetened)
- Cottage cheese (low-fat)
- Almond milk (unsweetened)

### Grains and Legumes:

- Quinoa
- Brown Rice
- Lentils
- Chickpeas (canned)

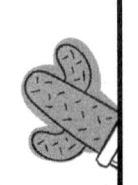

### Pantry Essentials:

- Olive oil (extra virgin)
- Coconut oil
- Balsamic vinegar
- Lime juice
- Sea salt
- Paprika
- Ground cumin
- Ground coriander
- Ground turmeric
- Ground black pepper
- Marinara sauce (unsweetened)

### Nuts and Seeds:

- Walnuts
- Flaxseeds

### Frozen:

- Edamame

### Miscellaneous:

- Hummus (store-bought or ingredients to make your own)
- Almond butter (unsweetened)
- Dark chocolate (for optional dark chocolate drizzle on macaroons)

### Optional:

- Stevia or other sugar substitute (for sweetening chia pudding or desserts)
- Ensure to check your pantry for any items you already have on hand before heading to the store. This list is comprehensive for the week's meal plan, providing you with everything you need to prepare nutritious meals while managing your diabetes effectively.

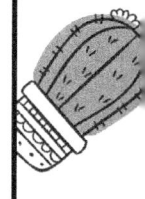

# Prep Tips: How to Efficiently Prepare Meals in Advance

Efficient meal preparation is a cornerstone of successful diabetes management, ensuring that nutritious meals are readily available, reducing the temptation for less healthy options. Here are practical tips to help you streamline your meal prep process:

1. Plan Your Meals Ahead

Begin by planning your meals for the week. Referencing your chosen recipes from the provided list ensures variety and adherence to nutritional goals. Consider including a mix of proteins, whole grains, vegetables, and healthy fats to promote balanced blood sugar levels throughout the day.

2. Make a Detailed Shopping List

Once your meal plan is set, compile a comprehensive shopping list based on the ingredients required for each recipe. Organise the list by categories (produce, proteins, pantry items, etc.) to make shopping quicker and more efficient. Check your pantry to avoid unnecessary purchases.

3. Batch Cooking Basics

Batch cooking involves preparing larger quantities of food in advance, which can be portioned and stored for later use.
Here is how to do it effectively:

- » Choose a Dedicated Time: Schedule a block of time each week for batch cooking. This could be a weekend afternoon or any time that suits your schedule.
- » Focus on Staples: Cook large batches of grains (like quinoa or brown rice), proteins (chicken breast, turkey meatballs), and vegetables (roasted broccoli, sautéed spinach). These staples can be used in multiple recipes throughout the week.
- » Portion Control: After cooking, portion the food into individual meal containers. This not only makes meals easy to grab and reheat but also helps control portion sizes, which is crucial for managing blood sugar levels.

4. Use Efficient Cooking Methods

Opt for cooking methods that require less firsthand time or allow for multitasking:
- » One-Pan Meals: Recipes that can be prepared in a single pan or sheet pan minimise clean-up and simplify the cooking process.
- » Slow Cooker or Instant Pot: These appliances are ideal for cooking soups, stews, or proteins with minimal effort. Set it and forget it until mealtime.
- » Grilling or Baking: Both grilling and baking are healthy cooking methods that require less oil compared to frying. Prepare batches of grilled chicken or baked fish to use throughout the week.

5. Prep Fresh Ingredients

Prep fresh ingredients in advance to save time during the week:

- » Wash and Chop Vegetables: Wash and chop vegetables as soon as you bring them home from the store. Store them in airtight containers or zip-top bags for easy access when cooking.
- » Prep Smoothie Packs: If you enjoy breakfast smoothies, pre-pack smoothie ingredients into individual bags or containers and store them in the freezer. This allows for quick blending in the morning.

6. Store Meals Properly

Proper storage is essential for maintaining food safety and quality:

- » Refrigerate or Freeze: Divide cooked meals into individual containers and store them in the refrigerator for up to 3-4 days. For longer storage, freeze meals and thaw them overnight in the refrigerator before reheating.
- » Label and Date: Use labels to identify the contents and date of preparation. This helps track freshness and avoid food waste.

7. Rotate Recipes

To keep meals interesting and balanced, rotate through different recipes each week. Use seasonal produce and adjust recipes to fit your preferences and nutritional needs.

8. Stay Organised

Maintain an organised kitchen to streamline meal prep:

- » Keep Essential Tools Handy: Gather utensils, cutting boards, and containers you use frequently. This minimises time spent searching for items during meal preparation.
- » Clean as You Go: Wash dishes and wipe down countertops as you cook to maintain a clean and functional workspace.

9. Safety First

Practice safe food handling and storage practices to prevent contamination and ensure food safety:

- » Thaw Safely: Thaw frozen foods in the refrigerator or microwave, not on the countertop, to prevent bacterial growth.
- » Use Proper Storage Containers: Choose containers that are microwave-safe and freezer-safe. Avoid using plastic containers that are scratched or worn out.

10. Enjoy the Benefits

Efficient meal prep not only supports better blood sugar management but also saves time and reduces stress during busy weekdays. Experiment with different recipes and meal prep techniques to find what works best for your lifestyle and dietary preferences.

By incorporating these meal prep tips into your routine, you can maintain a balanced diet while managing diabetes effectively, making healthy eating sustainable and enjoyable.

# 8 - LIFESTYLE TIPS FOR DIABETICS

## Exercise and Fitness: Incorporating Physical Activity

Physical activity plays a crucial role in managing diabetes effectively, offering numerous health benefits beyond blood sugar control. Here is a comprehensive guide to incorporating exercise into your lifestyle as a diabetic:

### Understanding the Benefits

Regular physical activity is essential for managing diabetes because it helps:

- Control Blood Sugar Levels: Exercise enhances insulin sensitivity, allowing cells to use blood sugar more effectively.
- Manage Weight: Maintaining a healthy weight reduces insulin resistance and lowers the risk of complications.
- Improve Cardiovascular Health: Exercise strengthens the heart and improves circulation, reducing the risk of heart disease, a common complication of diabetes.
- Boost Mood and Energy Levels: Physical activity releases endorphins, which can improve mood and reduce stress, both beneficial for overall well-being.

### Types of Exercise

Diabetics can benefit from a variety of exercises, including:

- Aerobic Exercise: Activities like walking, jogging, cycling, swimming, and dancing improve cardiovascular fitness and help control blood sugar levels.
- Strength Training: Resistance exercises using weights or resistance bands build muscle mass, improve metabolism, and aid in managing blood sugar.
- Flexibility and Balance Exercises: Stretching, yoga, and tai chi enhance flexibility, reduce stress, and improve overall well-being.

### Creating an Exercise Plan

Developing a personalised exercise plan involves:

- Consulting with Healthcare Providers: Before starting any exercise regimen, consult with your healthcare team to ensure safety and address any specific considerations related to diabetes management.
- Setting Realistic Goals: Establish achievable goals based on your current fitness level and health status. Gradually increase the intensity and duration of exercise over time.
- Choosing Activities You Enjoy: Select activities that you find enjoyable and are more likely to incorporate into your daily routine.

## Incorporating Exercise into Daily Life

To make physical activity a regular part of your routine:

- » Schedule Regular Sessions: Aim for at least 150 minutes of moderate-intensity aerobic activity per week, spread over at least three days, with no more than two consecutive days without exercise.
- » Break it Down: If time is limited, divide activity into shorter sessions throughout the day, such as 10-minute walks after meals.
- » Include Strength Training: Incorporate resistance exercises at least two days per week, targeting major muscle groups.

## Tips for Safe Exercise

For safe and effective exercise with diabetes:

- » Monitor Blood Sugar Levels: Check blood sugar before and after exercise, especially if you are on insulin or certain medications that can lower blood sugar.
- » Stay Hydrated: Drink water before, during, and after exercise to prevent dehydration.
- » Wear Proper Footwear: Choose supportive footwear to prevent foot problems, a common concern for diabetics.
- » Listen to Your Body: Stop activity if you experience dizziness, chest pain, or other unusual symptoms. Always seek medical advice if you have concerns.

## Integrating Exercise with Diabetes Management

Exercise complements other aspects of diabetes care:

- » Nutrition: Maintain a balanced diet that supports physical activity, providing adequate fuel before and after workouts.
- » Medication Management: Adjust medication dosages as needed with guidance from healthcare providers to account for changes in physical activity levels.

## Monitoring Progress

Track your progress to stay motivated and adjust as necessary:

- » Keep a Log: Record your exercise sessions, including type, duration, and intensity. Note any changes in blood sugar levels and how you feel during and after exercise.
- » Celebrate Achievements: Celebrate milestones, such as increased stamina or weight loss, to maintain motivation and reinforce healthy habits.

# Stress Management: Techniques for Reducing Stress

Stress management is crucial for individuals living with diabetes, as stress can directly impact blood sugar levels and overall health. Here are effective techniques to help reduce stress and improve well-being:

## **Understanding Stress and Diabetes**

Stress triggers the release of hormones like cortisol and adrenaline, which can raise blood sugar levels. Long-term stress can also affect insulin sensitivity and lead to unhealthy coping mechanisms such as overeating or skipping medications.
Managing stress effectively is therefore essential for diabetes management.

## **Techniques for Reducing Stress**

1. Regular Physical Activity:

Engage in regular exercise, such as walking, yoga, or swimming, to reduce stress hormones and promote relaxation. Physical activity also improves mood through the release of endorphins.

2. Deep Breathing and Relaxation Exercises:

Practice deep breathing techniques or progressive muscle relaxation to calm the mind and body. Set aside a few minutes daily for these exercises to alleviate stress.

3. Mindfulness and Meditation:

Incorporate mindfulness practices into your daily routine, such as mindful eating or meditation. Mindfulness helps focus attention on the present moment, reducing anxiety and stress.

4. Healthy Sleep Habits:

Prioritise quality sleep by maintaining a regular sleep schedule and creating a relaxing bedtime routine. Sufficient sleep supports overall health and resilience against stress.

5. Social Support:

Connect with friends, family, or support groups to share experiences and receive emotional support. Talking to others can provide perspective and reduce feelings of isolation.

6. Time Management:

Organise tasks and priorities to reduce overwhelm. Break down larger tasks into smaller, manageable steps and delegate when possible, to avoid stress from feeling overloaded.

7. Hobbies and Relaxing Activities:

Engage in hobbies or activities you enjoy, such as reading, gardening, or listening to music. Taking time for pleasurable activities can reduce stress and promote a sense of fulfilment.

8. Limiting Stimulants:

Reduce intake of stimulants like caffeine and nicotine, which can exacerbate feelings of anxiety and stress. Opt for herbal teas or decaffeinated beverages instead.

9. Cognitive Behavioural Techniques:

Use cognitive behavioural therapy (CBT) techniques to challenge negative thought patterns and develop healthier coping strategies for managing stress.

## **Integrating Stress Management with Diabetes Care**

- » Consistent Self-Care Routine: Incorporate stress management techniques into your daily self-care routine alongside monitoring blood sugar levels, taking medications as prescribed, and maintaining a balanced diet.
- » Monitoring Stress Levels: Track stress triggers and responses using a journal or app. Recognising patterns can help identify effective strategies for managing stress effectively.
- » Seek Professional Support: Consult with healthcare providers or therapists if stress becomes overwhelming or interferes with diabetes management. They can provide tailored guidance and support.

# Monitoring Progress: Keeping Track of Health Metrics

Monitoring health metrics is crucial for individuals with diabetes to assess their progress, manage their condition effectively, and make informed decisions about their health. Here is a comprehensive guide on monitoring key health metrics:

## **Importance of Monitoring Health Metrics**

1. Blood Glucose Levels:

Regular monitoring of blood glucose levels (both fasting and postprandial) helps individuals understand how food, physical activity, medications, and stress impact their blood sugar levels. This information enables adjustments to treatment plans to achieve optimal glucose control.

2. HbA1c Levels:

The HbA1c test provides a snapshot of average blood sugar levels over the past 2-3 months. It is a crucial indicator of long-term glucose control and helps healthcare providers assess diabetes management effectiveness. Aim for target HbA1c levels recommended by your healthcare team.

3. Blood Pressure:

High blood pressure (hypertension) is common among individuals with diabetes and increases the risk of cardiovascular complications. Regular blood pressure monitoring helps detect changes early, allowing for timely interventions through lifestyle modifications or medications.

4. Cholesterol Levels:

Monitoring cholesterol levels, including LDL (bad cholesterol), HDL (good cholesterol), and triglycerides, is essential as diabetes increases the risk of heart disease. Healthy cholesterol levels contribute to cardiovascular health and overall well-being.

5. Body Weight and BMI:

Monitoring body weight and calculating Body Mass Index (BMI) helps individuals understand their weight status and assess whether lifestyle changes are needed to achieve and maintain a healthy weight. Excess weight can impact insulin sensitivity and overall health.

6. Kidney Function (Microalbuminuria):

Diabetes can affect kidney function over time. Monitoring kidney health through tests like microalbuminuria (urine test for protein) helps detect early signs of kidney damage, enabling initiative-taking management and prevention of complications.

## **Tools for Monitoring Health Metrics**

- » Blood Glucose Meters: Portable devices used to measure blood sugar levels. Record results regularly and share them with your healthcare provider during check-ups.
- » Continuous Glucose Monitoring (CGM) Systems: CGM systems provide real-time glucose readings throughout the day and night. They help identify trends and patterns in blood sugar levels, guiding adjustments to diabetes management strategies.
- » Blood Pressure Monitors: Home blood pressure monitors allow individuals to track their blood pressure regularly. Follow instructions for accurate measurements and share results with healthcare providers.
- » Cholesterol Tests: Lipid profile tests measure cholesterol levels in the blood. Schedule regular tests as recommended by healthcare providers to monitor cholesterol levels and assess cardiovascular risk.
- » Digital Health Apps: Use diabetes management apps to log blood glucose readings, track food intake, record physical activity, and set reminders for medications. These apps provide a comprehensive view of diabetes management efforts.

## **Establishing a Monitoring Routine**

1. Set Goals: Work with healthcare providers to set specific, achievable goals for blood glucose, HbA1c, blood pressure, cholesterol, weight, and other relevant metrics.

2. Create a Monitoring Schedule: Develop a routine for monitoring health metrics based on healthcare provider recommendations. Regularity ensures consistency and accurate assessment of progress.

3. Track Trends and Patterns: Review recorded data regularly to identify trends and patterns in health metrics. Note any deviations from target ranges and discuss them with healthcare providers for adjustments to treatment plans.

4. Use Technology Wisely: Embrace technology like mobile apps and wearable devices to simplify monitoring and improve engagement in diabetes self-care.

## **Integrating Monitoring with Diabetes Management**

- » Educational Support: Attend diabetes education sessions to learn about the importance of monitoring health metrics and gain practical skills for effective self-management.
- » Regular Check-ups: Schedule regular check-ups with healthcare providers to review monitored metrics, discuss progress towards goals, and receive personalised guidance on diabetes management.
- » Self-Reflection and Adjustment: Reflect on monitored data to assess lifestyle factors influencing health metrics. Make informed adjustments to diet, exercise, medication adherence, and stress management techniques to achieve optimal diabetes control.

# CONCLUSION

Embarking on a journey to manage diabetes through diet and lifestyle changes is both empowering and challenging. It requires dedication, education, and a continuous source of motivation. Here, I offer essential encouragement and support strategies to help you stay motivated and committed to your health goals.

## Understanding the Importance of Support

Support is a cornerstone of successful diabetes management. It comes in various forms – from healthcare professionals and family members to peer support groups and online communities. Recognising and using these resources can significantly enhance your ability to maintain a healthy lifestyle.

## Building a Support Network

1. Healthcare Team:

   » Diabetes Specialist: Your endocrinologist or diabetes specialist is your primary resource for medical guidance. Regular consultations ensure your treatment plan is effective and adjusted as needed.
   » Dietitian/Nutritionist: These professionals provide personalised dietary advice and meal planning tips to help you make informed food choices.
   » Diabetes Educator: Certified diabetes educators offer practical education on managing blood glucose levels, using monitoring devices, and integrating diabetes care into daily life.

2. Family and Friends:

   » Involvement: Involve your loved ones in your journey by educating them about diabetes and its management. Their understanding and support can make a significant difference.
   » Encouragement: Lean on family and friends for emotional support. Share your progress and challenges with them and celebrate your successes together.

3. Peer Support Groups:

   » Local Groups: Join local diabetes support groups to connect with others who share similar experiences. These groups offer a sense of community and an opportunity to exchange tips and encouragement.
   » Online Communities: Participate in online forums and social media groups dedicated to diabetes management. These platforms provide a space for sharing stories, asking questions, and receiving advice from a broad community.

# **Staying Motivated: Practical Tips**

1. Set Realistic Goals:

   » Short-Term Goals: Break down your long-term health objectives into smaller, achievable steps. This makes progress tangible and provides a sense of accomplishment.
   » Celebrate Milestones: Acknowledge and celebrate when you reach milestones, no matter how small. Positive reinforcement boosts motivation.

2. Track Your Progress:

   » Journaling: Keep a daily journal to record your meals, physical activity, blood glucose levels, and feelings. Reviewing your entries can highlight progress and areas for improvement.
   » Apps and Gadgets: Use diabetes management apps and wearable devices to track your health metrics.
   These tools provide visual progress reports and reminders to stay on track.

3. Educate Yourself:

   » Continuous Learning: Stay informed about diabetes by reading books, attending workshops, and following reputable health websites. Knowledge empowers you to make better decisions and stay engaged in your care.
   » Recipes and Cooking: Experiment with new diabetic-friendly recipes to keep your meals exciting and prevent dietary monotony.

4. Mindfulness and Stress Management:

   » Mindfulness Practices: Incorporate mindfulness techniques such as meditation, deep breathing exercises, and yoga into your routine. These practices reduce stress and improve overall well-being.
   » Stress Management: Identify and manage stressors in your life. Chronic stress can negatively impact blood sugar levels and overall health. Seek professional help if needed.

5. Physical Activity:

   » Regular Exercise: Engage in regular physical activity that you enjoy. Exercise improves insulin sensitivity, aids weight management, and boosts mood.
   » Variety: Incorporate a variety of activities such as walking, swimming, cycling, or strength training to keep your routine interesting and effective.

## **Encouragement for the Journey Ahead**

Managing diabetes is a lifelong journey that requires perseverance and adaptability. Remember that every small step you take towards a healthier lifestyle is a victory. Surround yourself with supportive individuals and use available resources to stay motivated.

# APPENDICES

## Basics Glossary of Terms for the Diabetic Diet

Understanding the terminology associated with a diabetic diet is crucial for managing diabetes effectively. This glossary is designed to familiarise beginners with key terms and concepts that will aid in making informed dietary choices.

### A

A1C (HbA1c): A blood test that measures average blood glucose levels over the past two to three months. It is a crucial indicator of diabetes management, with a lower A1C reflecting better control.

Artificial Sweeteners: Non-nutritive sweeteners used as a substitute for sugar. Examples include aspartame, saccharin, and stevia, which do not raise blood glucose levels.

### B

Blood Glucose (Blood Sugar): The amount of glucose present in the blood. Maintaining stable blood glucose levels is vital for people with diabetes.

Body Mass Index (BMI): A measure of body fat based on height and weight. A healthy BMI is important for diabetes management and overall health.

### C

Carbohydrates (Carbs): Nutrients that provide energy. Carbohydrates have a direct impact on blood glucose levels and are classified into simple and complex carbs. Monitoring carb intake is essential for managing diabetes.

Carbohydrate Counting: A method used to manage blood glucose levels by tracking the number of carbohydrates consumed in each meal and snack.

Continuous Glucose Monitor (CGM): A device that continuously tracks blood glucose levels throughout the day and night, providing real-time data and trends.

Complex Carbohydrates: Carbohydrates that are made up of long chains of sugar molecules. They are found in foods such as whole grains, vegetables, and legumes and are digested more slowly, leading to a gradual rise in blood glucose.

C-peptide: A substance made in the pancreas, along with insulin. Measuring C-peptide levels can help determine how much insulin the body is producing.

## D

Dawn Phenomenon: An early-morning increase in blood glucose levels due to the release of hormones such as cortisol and adrenaline.

Diabetes Mellitus: A group of diseases characterised by high blood glucose levels. It includes Type 1 diabetes, Type 2 diabetes, and gestational diabetes.

Dietary Fibre: A type of carbohydrate that the body cannot digest. Fibre helps regulate blood glucose levels and promotes a healthy digestive system.

## E

Exchange Lists: A meal planning system that groups foods into categories based on their carbohydrate, protein, and fat content. It helps in managing portions and balancing meals.

## F

Fructose: A natural sugar found in fruits and honey. Unlike glucose, fructose does not cause a rapid rise in blood glucose levels but should still be consumed in moderation.

## G

Glycaemic Index (GI): A ranking of carbohydrate-containing foods based on their effect on blood glucose levels. Foods with a low GI cause a slower, more gradual rise in blood glucose.

Glycaemic Load (GL): A measure that considers the GI of a food and the amount of carbohydrate in a serving. It provides a more comprehensive understanding of a food's impact on blood glucose.

## H

Hyperglycaemia: High blood glucose levels. Symptoms include excessive thirst, frequent urination, and fatigue. Managing hyperglycaemia is crucial to prevent complications.

Hypoglycaemia: Low blood glucose levels. Symptoms include sweating, shaking, confusion, and irritability. Quick treatment with glucose tablets or sugary foods is necessary.

## I

Insulin: A hormone produced by the pancreas that helps regulate blood glucose levels by allowing glucose to enter cells. People with Type 1 diabetes and some with Type 2 diabetes may require insulin injections.

Insulin Resistance: A condition where the body's cells do not respond effectively to insulin, leading to higher blood glucose levels. It is common in Type 2 diabetes.

## K

Ketones: Chemicals produced when the body breaks down fat for energy. High levels of ketones can lead to diabetic ketoacidosis, a serious complication.

## M

Macrovascular Complications: Diabetes-related complications that affect large blood vessels, including heart disease and stroke.

Microvascular Complications: Diabetes-related complications that affect small blood vessels, including retinopathy (eye disease), nephropathy (kidney disease), and neuropathy (nerve damage).

## N

Non-Starchy Vegetables: Vegetables low in carbohydrates, such as leafy greens, broccoli, and peppers. They have minimal impact on blood glucose levels and are rich in nutrients.

## P

Pancreas: The organ that produces insulin. In Type 1 diabetes, the pancreas does not produce insulin, while in Type 2 diabetes, the body becomes resistant to insulin or does not produce enough.

Polydipsia: Excessive thirst, a common symptom of diabetes. Polyuria: Frequent urination, a common symptom of diabetes. S
Self-Monitoring of Blood Glucose (SMBG): The practice of regularly checking blood glucose levels using a glucose meter. It helps in managing diabetes by providing immediate feedback.

Starch: A type of complex carbohydrate found in foods such as potatoes, bread, and pasta. Starches can raise blood glucose levels and should be eaten in moderation.

## T

Type 1 Diabetes: An autoimmune condition where the body's immune system attacks the insulin-producing cells in the pancreas. It requires lifelong insulin therapy.

Type 2 Diabetes: A condition where the body becomes resistant to insulin or does not produce enough. It is often managed with lifestyle changes, oral medications, and sometimes insulin.

## V

Visceral Fat: Fat stored around internal organs. High levels of visceral fat are associated with increased risk of Type 2 diabetes and other health issues.

# Measurement Conversions for the Diabetic Diet: A Beginner's Guide for the UK

Embarking on a diabetic diet involves not only understanding what to eat but also how to measure and convert various ingredients accurately. This guide is designed to help beginners in the UK navigate the essential measurement conversions, ensuring you can follow recipes accurately and manage your diabetes effectively.

## Understanding Measurements

In the UK, we commonly use both metric (grams, millilitres) and imperial (ounces, pints) measurements. Familiarising yourself with these systems and knowing how to convert between them is crucial for accurate portion control and dietary management.

## Common Conversions

Weight:

- 1 ounce (oz) = 28 grams (g)
- 1 pound (lb) = 454 grams (g)
- 100 grams (g) = 3.5 ounces (oz)

Volume:

- 1 teaspoon (tsp) = 5 millilitres (ml)
- 1 tablespoon (tbsp) = 15 millilitres (ml)
- 1 fluid ounce (fl oz) = 30 millilitres (ml)
- 1 cup (UK) = 240 millilitres (ml)
- 1 pint (UK) = 568 millilitres (ml)

Length:

- 1 inch = 2.54 centimetres (cm)

## Practical Applications in Cooking

Measuring Ingredients:

Accurate measurement of ingredients is vital, especially for those managing diabetes. Here is how to measure common ingredients:

- Flour and Sugar: Use a flat knife to level off the top after scooping into the measuring cup.
- Liquids: Use a clear measuring jug for liquids, checking at eye level for precision.
- Herbs and Spices: Measure dried herbs and spices with measuring spoons, levelling off the excess for accuracy.

Using Scales:

Invest in a digital kitchen scale. Weighing ingredients is often more accurate than measuring by volume, particularly for solid foods like vegetables, meats, and grains.

## **Converting Recipes**

When following recipes, especially those from international sources, conversion can be essential. Here is how to adapt a recipe using the above conversions:

Example Recipe Conversion:

A US recipe calls for 1 cup of flour, 1 tablespoon of sugar, and 1 cup of milk.

- Flour: 1 cup = 240 ml. Since flour is a dry ingredient, it converts to approximately 120 grams.
- Sugar: 1 tablespoon = 15 ml. For sugar, this converts to approximately 12.5 grams.
- Milk: 1 cup = 240 ml (same in UK measurements).

## **Portion Control**

Accurate measurement supports portion control, a critical aspect of managing diabetes. Here are some tips:

- Plate Method: Divide your plate into sections – half for non-starchy vegetables, a quarter for lean protein, and a quarter for whole grains or starchy vegetables.
- Hand Method: Use your hand to estimate portions – a fist-sized portion for carbohydrates, a palm-sized portion for protein, and a thumb-sized portion for fats.

## **Enhancing Flavours Without Extra Sugars**

Use fresh herbs, spices, and citrus to add flavour without adding sugar or sodium. Experiment with combinations like:

- Herbs: Basil, coriander, rosemary, thyme
- Spices: Cumin, paprika, turmeric, cinnamon
- Citrus: Lemon or lime zest and juice

## **Tips for Meal Planning and Carbohydrate Counting**

Meal planning helps in managing blood glucose levels. When planning meals:

- Balance Macronutrients: Include carbohydrates, proteins, and fats in every meal.
- Carbohydrate Counting: Aim for consistent carbohydrate intake at each meal. Use the conversion of grams to understand the carbohydrate content of different foods.
- Glycaemic Index: Choose low-GI foods to maintain stable blood glucose levels.

# **Sample Conversion for a Diabetic-Friendly Recipe**

Original Recipe:

- 2 cups of cooked quinoa
- 1/2 cup of diced cucumber
- 1/4 cup of feta cheese

Converted Recipe (UK):

- 2 cups quinoa = 480 ml (approx. 340 grams cooked quinoa)
- 1/2 cup cucumber = 120 ml (approx. 75 grams diced cucumber)
- 1/4 cup feta cheese = 60 ml (approx. 40 grams feta cheese)

Dear Reader,

Thank you for choosing "Diabetic Cookbook for Beginners"! Your feedback is invaluable to me. I would really appreciate it if you could take a moment to leave a review of your experience with my cookbook.

Simply scan the QR code below to be directed to the review page. Or go to this webpage:

https://www.amazon.co.uk/dp/B0DDVSN5X1

Your honest review will help me continue to improve and provide the best resources for my readers.

Thank you for your support!

Warm regards,

Aurora August

# Index

Symbols

1 - Getting Started 15
2 - Breakfast Boosters 23
4 - Nutritious Dinner 48
5 – Smart Snacking 60
6 – Delightful Desserts 72
7 - Meal Planning And Prep 84
8 - Lifestyle Tips For Diabetics 91
30 Food That Must Be Banned Or Limited For Diabetics 21

A

About The Author 109
Almond Flour Chocolate Chip Cookie 79
Appendices 99
Apple Slices With Almond Butter 63
Avocado And Spinach Smoothie 33

B

Baked Apple With Cinnamon And Walnuts 75
Baked Cod With Roasted Brussels Sprouts 54
Baked Kale Chips With Sea Salt 67
Baked Salmon With Asparagus And Quinoa 50
Baked Sweet Potato With Greek Yoghurt And Chives 44
Balancing Macronutrients: Protein, Carbs, And Fats 35
Basics Glossary Of Terms For The Diabetic Diet 99
Bell Pepper Slices With Guacamole 71
Berry Crumble With Oats And Almonds 80

C

Celery Sticks With Cottage Cheese 66
Cherry Tomatoes And Mozzarella Balls 70
Chia Seed Breakfast Bowl 34
Chia Seed Pudding With Coconut Milk 76
Chicken And Vegetable Stir-Fry 46
Chickpea And Tuna Salad With Lemon Vinaigrette 43
Coconut Macaroons With Dark Chocolate Drizzle 82
Conclusion 97
Copyright Statement: 2
Core Principles Of The Diabetic Diet 8
Cottage Cheese And Berry Parfait 29
Cultural And Historical Background 10

D

Dark Chocolate Avocado Mousse 74
Disclaimer: 2

E

Edamame With A Sprinkle Of Sea Salt 69
Encouragement And Motivation 13
Exercise And Fitness: Incorporating Physical Activity 91

G

Greek Yoghurt With Nuts And Fresh 27
Greek Yoghurt With Walnuts And Fresh Berries 64
Grilled Chicken Salad With Mixed Greens And Vinaigrette 38

Grilled Chicken With Steamed Broccoli And Brown Rice 51

## H

Healthy Snack Options: Managing Cravings 60
Herb-Crusted Pork Tenderloin With Green Beans 57
Hummus With Cucumber And Carrot Sticks 62

## I

Importance Of Adopting The Diabetic Diet 12
Introduction 6

## L

Lean Beef Stir-Fry With Bell Peppers And Snow Peas 56
Lentil And Vegetable Soup 41

## M

Measurement Conversions For The Diabetic Diet: A Beginner's Guide For The Uk 102
Mixed Nuts And Dried Unsweetened Berries 68
Monitoring Progress: Keeping Track Of Health Metrics 95
Moving Forward 22

## O

Oatmeal With Flaxseeds And Blueberries 31
Opening Statement 6

## P

Pantry Basics - Stocking Diabetic-Friendly Ingredients 16
Pears Poached In Red Wine With A Cinnamon Stick 83
Planning Balanced Meals: Strategies For Dinner 48
Prep Tips: How To Efficiently Prepare Meals In Advance 88
Pumpkin Spice Energy Balls 81
Purpose Of The Diabetic Diet 6

## Q

Quinoa And Black Bean Salad With Lime Dressing 39
Quinoa Bowl With Berries And Nuts 28

## R

Raspberry Yoghurt Popsicles 78
Reading Labels - Understanding Nutritional Information 19
Roasted Chickpeas With Paprika 65

## S

Scrambled Tofu With Vegetables 25
Shopping List 86
Smoked Salmon And Cucumber Roll-Ups 32
Spaghetti Squash With Marinara And Turkey Meat Sauce 59
Spinach And Mushroom Stuffed Bell Peppers 42
Stir-Fried Tofu With Mixed Vegetables 52
Stress Management: Techniques For Reducing Stress 93

Stuffed Portobello Mushrooms With Spinach And Cheese 58
Sugar Alternatives: Using Sweeteners Wisely 72
Sugar-Free Lemon Cheesecake Bites 77

T

Tomato And Basil Soup With A Side Of Whole Grain Bread 47
Turkey And Avocado Lettuce Wraps 40
Turkey Meatballs With Zucchini Noodles 53

U

Understanding The Importance Of Support 97

V

Vegetable Curry With Cauliflower Rice 55
Vegetable Omelette With Mushrooms And Bell Peppers 30

W

Weekly Meal Plans: Sample Plans For Beginners 84
Whole Grain Toast With Smashed Avocado And Tomatoes 26
Why Breakfast Matters: Importance Of A Healthy Start 23

Z

Zucchini Noodles With Pesto And Cherry Tomatoes 45

Printed in Great Britain
by Amazon